Appraisal & Evaluation Library

Text-based Information Management Systems Volume

July 1991

London: HMSO

Appraisal and Evaluation Library
Text-based Information Management Systems Volume

© **Crown Copyright 1991**

First Published 1991
Applications for reproduction should be made to HMSO

ISBN 0 11 330571 0

For further information regarding this document please contact :-

Strategic Programmes Division
CCTA, Norwich
0603 694706

Foreword

This document is the Text-based Information Management Systems volume of the CCTA's Appraisal and Evaluation Library. This Library is intended to aid appraisal and evaluation of software products and consists of an Overview and Procedures volume, together with supporting technology specific volumes.

The Overview and Procedures volume describes the series and provides a procedure for using the criteria contained in the technology specific volumes in a number of contexts. These include making a strategic selection, evaluation during a feasibility study, and evaluation during the procurement stage of a project. The evaluation procedure is placed into the context of other CCTA procedures, such as those for procurement and evaluation, and methods such as SSADM. It has been written in support of the CCTA Information Systems Guides.

Each technology specific volume provides a hierarchy of criteria that may be used as the basis for the evaluation of products in that technology class. The initial volumes were for Database Management Systems and Application Generators. This volume on Text-based Information Management Systems joins the library accompanied by a volume on Knowledge Based Systems.

This Appraisal and Evaluation Library has been produced to assist organisations to identify the product, or set of products, which best meets their requirements. The procedure and the criteria have developed as technology has changed, and as a result of experience gained from their use. CCTA welcomes comment on, and contributions to, this Library to ensure that it continues to provide maximum benefit.

Appraisal and Evaluation Library
Text-based Information Management Systems Volume

Contents

	Introduction	page
i	General	9
ii	Scope	13
iii	Criteria	21

Chapter

1	**Text storage**	25
	1.1 General requirements	25
	1.2 Narrative forms	26
	1.3 DBMS extensions	32
	1.4 Compound documents	34
	1.5 Storage requirements and equipment	36
2	**Text retrieval**	41
	2.1 General requirements	41
	2.2 Retrieval aids	42
	2.3 Narrative records	47
	2.4 DBMS based systems	60
	2.5 Compound documents	62
3	**Text and document acquisition**	65
	3.1 Sources on paper	65
	3.2 Sources in computers	67
	3.3 Parsing requirements	68
	3.4 TIMS maintenance	70
4	**Reports and presentation methods**	75
	4.1 Report writers	75
	4.2 Indexes	77
	4.3 OA and DTP systems	78
5	**Performance**	81
	5.1 Serviceability	81
	5.2 Interactive response	91
	5.3 Batch performance	94
	5.4 Application design	97

6		**Special applications**	**99**
	6.1	Office environments	100
	6.2	Libraries and information centres	102
	6.3	Records management	103
	6.4	Electronic publishing	103
	6.5	Micro-computers	104
7		**Recent technical developments**	**109**
	7.1	Hypertext	109
	7.2	'Intelligent' interface	110
	7.3	Signatures in VLDB	113
	7.4	Hardware searching	114
	7.5	High density media	117
8		**Control and Security**	**119**
	8.1	Ownership	119
	8.2	Control over access	119
	8.3	Security planning	121
9		**Portability**	**123**
	9.1	TIMS portability	123
	9.2	Data portability	123
	9.3	Skill mobility	124
	9.4	Downloading	124
10		**Product credibility**	**127**
	10.1	Product quality	127
	10.2	Product development	128
	10.3	Supplier assessment	128
	10.4	Product background	130
	10.5	Documentation	133
	10.6	Training	134
	10.7	Support	135
	10.8	Enhancements	137
11		**Application development**	**139**
	11.1	TIMS in general	139
	11.2	DBMS aspects	141
	11.3	Development cycle support	145
	11.4	Application documentation	145
	11.5	Data conversion, loading, and migration tools	146
12		**Project specific requirements**	**149**

Contents

13	**Costs**		151
	13.1	Software	151
	13.2	Hardware	152
	13.3	System development operation and maintenance	152
	13.4	People costs	153
Annex A	**Criteria hierarchy**		155
Annex B	**Sources of further information**		163

Appraisal and Evaluation Library
Text-based Information Management Systems Volume

i General

i.1 Background

This document is the technology specific volume on Text-based Information Management Systems (TIMS) from the CCTA Appraisal and Evaluation Library of volumes on the subject of application development product appraisal and evaluation.

The objective of this Library is to define a framework for

> 'impartial and effective evaluation to find the product, or products, which best meet the needs and constraints of the organisation.'

The CCTA Information Systems Engineering Division first produced a guide to the Appraisal and Evaluation of Application Generator and Database Management System (DBMS) products in 1986. This document was updated in 1988, in the process being divided into two volumes, one for Application Generators and one for DBMS. The present volume extends the series to cover Text-based Information Management Systems in a similar format.

Several other subject areas have been identified where evaluation criteria may usefully be provided. To avoid duplication of content, the common procedural element, has been separated out into a separate Overview and Procedures volume as part of the Library.

The present volume provides evaluation criteria appropriate to TIMS products. It should be used in conjunction with the Overview and Procedures volume, and for certain applications as indicated in the following chapters, with the DBMS volume also.

i.2 The importance of TIMS

Text storage and retrieval products are becoming increasingly important, in particular because of a growing awareness of the large volumes of text-based information now available in electronic form. The acceptance of word processing, desktop publishing and the electronic exchange of information as normal tools of administration and technical management offers the opportunity to replace slow and space consuming traditional records and library systems with responsive, compact, interactive text databases.

Low cost mass storage development in the late 1980's has helped to create a systems environment for the success of TIMS products. Because software development has taken place in an increasingly competitive marketplace, with open procurement policies, implementors, as customers, have opportunities for wide choice.

i.3   **Audience**

The main audience for this document is Information Technology (IT) staff wishing to carry out appraisals or evaluations for soundly based procurement. It will also be of interest to senior IT management considering the introduction of text-based information management products and wishing to ensure that such introduction is carried out professionally, resulting in the selection of the most appropriate product.

It is assumed that the reader has at least a basic understanding of data processing, the role of recommended standard methods such as PRINCE and SSADM and of hardware architecture. Knowledge of text-based information management is not assumed, with introduction (ii) providing background information and explanation of the terminology used in this volume.

Because of these assumptions experienced TIMS practitioners may find the volume too descriptive in some parts, but technically simplified in others. It should be remembered, however, that the document will be used as a primer by those unfamiliar with the topic, and will also serve as a useful reference document for experienced people. Annex B provides a select list of references to the key literature on TIMS and related subjects for those who wish to follow up the topic in more depth.

i.4   **Expected uses**

It is expected that the volumes in this Library will be used in several ways. The uses identified in the Overview and Procedures Volume are:

- strategic, business-based, evaluation of products to select a 'standard' product for subsequent organisation wide use

- less detailed evaluation of products as an element of a feasibility study

- full evaluation of products during procurement for a project independent appraisal of a product.

i.5 **Structure** This document is in three parts - introductions, the evaluation criteria, and an annex.

This section introduces the volume as a whole. Introduction (ii) covers the scope of the subject area and explains the terminology. Introduction (iii) describes the notation used for the criteria, and summarises the main headings.

The bulk of the document contains the high level criteria and the checklists of detailed technical questions used within the evaluation model to assess and rank TIMS products. The questions may be used as an aide-memoire when gathering information about products.

The annex contains a hierarchy chart of the subject matter in this volume. This chart may be used as a default or as the basis for a hierarchy chart which best meets the needs of the project or organisation.

i.6 **Outline of the procedure**

The evaluation process comprises 7 stages which are described in the Overview and Procedures Volume.

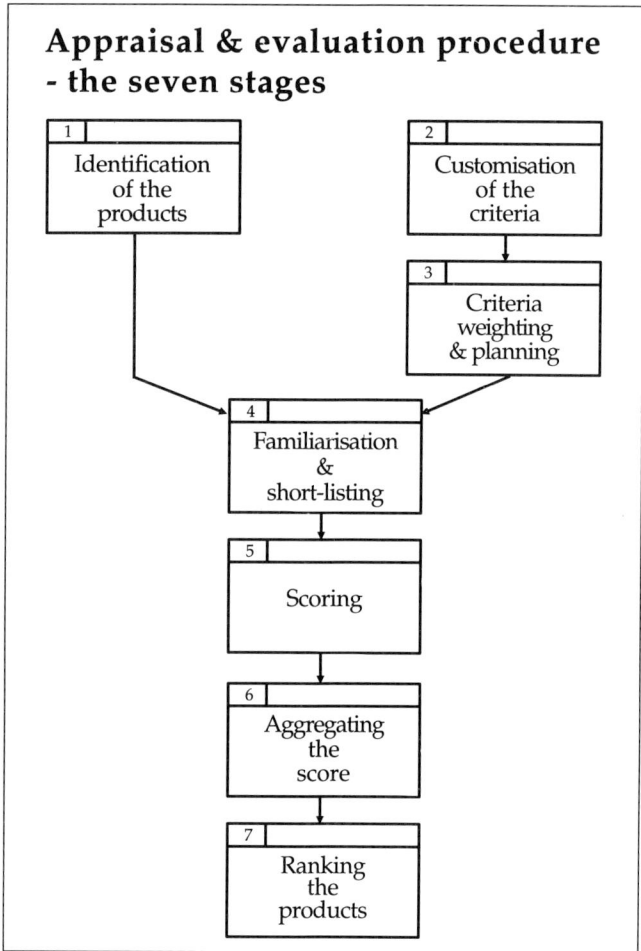

i.7 **History**

This, the first issue of the TIMS volume, has been written for CCTA by John Ashford. It has been designed in the light of experience gained with previous volumes in this series on Database Management Systems and on Application Generators. In particular, to make the current Appraisal and Evaluation volumes easier to use, it has been found helpful to intersperse detailed technical questions among the criteria.

ii Scope

ii.1 Scope of the volume

The evaluation criteria in this volume relate to Text-based Information Management System (TIMS) software products. Most of the content is concerned with multi-user systems, but the special needs of micro-computer based applications including single user systems and prototyping are considered in Chapter 6.

The term 'Text-based Information Management System' is used here to refer to those software products which are appropriate for the construction of databases where:

- a significant proportion of the information stored in the database is in the form of text in natural language;

- the text content is a necessary component of information retrieval, and is used to provide access to the records; and

- an interactive retrieval language is provided to allow query development and refinement by the user as a normal component of the applications of the database.

TIMS products have proved in practice to be very flexible, and have been applied to a wide range of text-related requirements including many aspects of library and information services. This scope is reflected in the criteria used in this volume, although it should be noted that dedicated and special purpose products narrowly directed to such areas as library house-keeping, records management, document production control, and expert systems for consultative applications are not considered in detail.

The evaluation method followed in this volume is particularly suited to, and has been used on, both strategic and tactical procurements. (See the Overview and Procedures Volume for further details.)

ii.2 Definitions Within the broad scope of Text-based Information Management Systems set out above, there are practical sub-divisions based on the completeness of the information presented, on the indexing and retrieval methodology employed, on the presence of non-text components and the way they are handled, and on the use of application-directed user interfaces. These sub-divisions are not exclusive, and any particular application involves a choice within each category. The following sections provide a brief guide to the classification of TIMS, and define many of the terms used later in the volume. For a more extended treatment, reference should be made to the sources listed in Annex B.

Full text and indicative text When the whole body of a text document is held within the TIMS database, and the view presented to the user is of the whole information about a subject as it is known to the system, this is referred to as a 'full text' (FTX) application. Typical cases are committee minutes, case reports, software documentation, where the whole body of the text contains useful access points for searching, and the user expects the full document to be delivered on-line.

In 'indicative text' (ITX) systems, the text record in the TIMS database is an intermediate 'pointer' to the full body of the record held elsewhere - in paper format, microfilm, or as an electronic image, but not within the text record proper. The traditional library catalogue is the classic example. In ITX systems document delivery may be a separate procedure entirely from identification that the document is 'wanted'.

Indexing strategy Text retrieval depends on the identification of words or phrases within natural language as the 'tokens' on which indexes will be set up and retrieval performed. Language may be widely defined, to include numbers, special character strings to indicate structure, ideographs in Chinese, Japanese and others, but in all cases a 'parser' is used to identify word and sentence breaks while text is being added to the database. In all cases except 'sequential' searching a separate index to the words ('tokens') in the database is built and stored as well as the original text file.

The simplest approach, 'sequential searching' makes no use of a separate index. For each user search request, the whole of the document file is scanned, looking for words or phrases which match those in the query. For small collections, and especially in ITX applications such as the 'profiles' of documents in word processor 'folders' this is simple, cheap and effective. In larger databases the search time increases linearly with database size, and rapidly becomes impracticable unless special purpose hardware (ICL CAFS, transputer farms - see Chapter 7.4) is used to speed up the scan.

The majority of commercial systems use an 'inverse file' (sometimes 'inverted file') approach to indexing. Here a file called a 'concordance' or 'word list' or 'vocabulary' is built up, in alphabetical order, of all of the words from the text which are wanted as index points. Unwanted words such as conjunctions and other frequently used words of little retrieval value may be discarded using a 'stop list' when new text is being added. For each word in the vocabulary, a pointer list is constructed showing the address of each record in which it occurs, and in many cases, the exact position within the record (section, paragraph, sentence, subdivisions are used). Searches are formed, directly or by a structured interface, as Boolean queries, using AND, OR and NOT operators, and the pointer lists for the query terms are combined using the Boolean operators to find a sub-set of the text records which satisfy the query. If references in the pointer lists are to exact word positions, then the direct searching for phrases and for words in close proximity is feasible. Otherwise a set of 'possible' records is retrieved, and reduced by sequential scanning to deal with phrases and 'proximity'.

A common alternative is to build the index not from the words in the text themselves, but from computed values which represent the words by a smaller number of 'bits' in a fixed length bit row which represents the whole document. The set of bit rows then represents all of the documents in the database as 'signatures', often taking up much less space than would the corresponding inverse file indexes. Searches are performed by forming a similar bit row for the terms in the search query, and sequentially matching the query row against the set of document rows looking for correspondences. A number of algorithms for performance improvement in storage and scanning of the bit rows have been published (Chapter 7.3). The range of facilities available to the user during retrieval is often restricted compared with inverse file systems, particularly in searching for 'truncated' words.

A fast, simple version of signature indexing for small databases with only a limited search vocabulary - say up to 2,000 key words - is to form the bit row by allocating a position for each word in the vocabulary, its plural, and maybe its grammatical stem. This gives very low index overhead and reasonably fast retrieval for this simple special case. and has been effectively applied to databases of news transcripts.

Data structures

It is convenient, though the boundaries are sometimes not too clear, to sub-divide text databases by the structure of the text records. This is a useful measure of the complexity of the tools and facilities which may be required of the TIMS software.

Narrative text contains only a minimum of extraneous codes and indicators. It is likely to include, especially in ITX applications, a number of 'section' or 'field' markers, which may or may not be visible to the user, and embedded data fields such as dates, quantities and reference numbers may have preceding identifiers. The text is typically the result of using 'ASCII' or 'TEXT' options for transfer of word processor files, and normally contains few special characters (é, ü, ô, \, ¶, æ, ≡ etc) or none.

Annotated text includes narrative text, and adds a wide range of mark-up and pointers to extend its structure and content. Text derived directly from word processors may incorporate many special and control characters, 'invisible' to the user. Publishers' manuscripts and internal records often nowadays contain SGML mark-up to define structures (Chapter 1.2). Line drawings and other vector graphics may be incorporated by the inclusion of 'pointers' in the narrative text, to show where the graphics file is stored. Spreadsheet data may be held and maintained externally, and transferred to the text database at the site of the pointer on demand. Non-roman scripts may be represented in dual native and romanised transcript versions. Tables and column structures within narrative text are a common presentation format, requiring more or less concealed mark-up depending on the TIMS product concerned.

Hybrid documents with inter-related text and images form a growing class of applications where annotations within the narrative point to sources of images - more text, or mixtures of text, graphics and half-tone illustrations, or even colour - and call implicit instructions for the presentation of the image material on the same, or an adjacent screen. Good applications have been found in archives, museum displays, and references databases for clinical medicine.

Database architectures

Two main database architectures have become established for text-based information management systems. The majority, referred to for convenience in this volume as 'traditional text' use inverse file indexing and a simple structure of some four main data files. The software provides its own file and record management, space control, access locking and recovery procedures. The main files are, typically:

- Text file of actual documents;

- Vocabulary or Word List or Concordance file;

- Pointer file of short lists or tables;

- Utility file or files for stop lists, macros, synonym storage, parking files, work space during pointer list processing, user work space (see later chapters for more details).

This architecture forms the basis for Chapters 1.2, 2.2 and 2.3 in particular. It is the form usually referred to in the general literature as 'text retrieval software'. Database back-up in batch mode is convenient, and batch restore after loss of the system is easy. Recovery to a coherent on-line state is much more difficult, and treatment of transient errors during interactive working is often problematic.

An occasional variation is to store the text not as a single file of complete records, but as a set of sub-files, one for each text field. For some retrieval strategies, this offers fast responses for simple queries, and is the structure adopted by several of the very large on-line bibliographic service vendors.

The main alternative to the traditional text database structure is to use a Database Management System (DBMS) and text storage and retrieval facilities for designated fields within the structured records, identified in this volume as '**DBMS+Text**'. Examples are found for all of the main classes of DBMS - hierarchic, network and relational - and for all of these the text extension is essentially similar. (For details of DBMS systems architectures and their appraisal see the Database Management Systems volume in this series.)

For each field designated as 'text' (or in relational databases, each text domain from which fields are drawn) an inverse file index is constructed, normally maintaining location pointers at file, record, and field level, sometimes at paragraph and sentence within the field and down to exact word location level. So far as the inverse file part is concerned it is similar to the traditional text database, but this is superimposed on the full structured database with all its facilities of recovery, rollback to a consistent state after a fault, record locking during update, transaction processing and others. Such systems gain from the addition of structured database features, but tend to be inflexible, more complicated to implement, and sometimes less efficient in performance on large data sets than the traditional text forms.

A third, much looser, '**compound**' architecture has been implemented in a number of applications where a traditional text database and a structured database have been coupled through 'gateways' in one or the other package. Each software product is more or less independent and quite varied pairings have been successfully used. The necessary facility is the gateway which allows a user of either package to suspend, temporarily, the current operation while preserving its status, and for an interlude access the other system. Fields or files may be transferred between the two systems. At the end of the interlude, the user returns to the suspended stage of the 'home' application and continues as before the interruption.

Such implementations are usually restricted to a particular operating system (Chapter 9). Compound architectures are often used in response to special applications (Chapter 6), and are best treated for selection criteria as if they were the sum of two requirements, together with a few specific aspects of the linkage and the fault recovery processes.

User interfaces

For some purposes it is useful to sub-divide applications on the basis of whether the user interacts directly with the retrieval software, or through an application program in which the text database calls have been embedded. There are also marked differences between user interfaces which are 'command line' based, maintaining a dialogue with the user; those which apply some variant of a 'form-filling' approach; and those which attempt, through 'artificial intelligence' or other procedures, to make the presentation at the interface dynamically responsive to the user's needs.

TIMS users are often not 'computer-literate', and in many cases the system is used by others than those for whom it was set up. This presents design challenges both for user interfaces and for training and 'help' structures.

Special formats

Signature systems, hardware based search engines, and some products which apply 'intelligent' user interfaces tend to use dedicated and special purpose data formats and system architectures. These products often require appraisal in detail during evaluation, and their suitability will be very dependent on their fitness for purpose under quite special criteria. Instances will occur, for example, under 'very large' databases

(Chapter 7). In the following chapters, notes will be found in appropriate places indicating the possibility that special formats may be involved, and if a project involves more than a few such aspects, then specialist advice should be sought.

iii Criteria

iii.1 Notation

The criteria in this volume are structured as a hierarchy, as shown in Annex A.

The main body of the text falls into three classes:

- the main discussion of the criteria - it is primarily this text that should be customised for particular projects against which weights are assigned and scores allotted. To obtain an overview of the criteria this text can be read in isolation. This is printed in 10 point Palatino typeface, that is, the one used to print this paragraph, alongside a numbered heading in bold type, as in the heading of this section. Where the criteria cover a large subject area they are divided into sub-criteria and are printed in the normal typeface with an unnumbered side heading in the same typeface.

- detailed discussion of the criteria or sub-criteria - this level is required for information gathering. This is also in the 10 point Palatino typeface and does not have headings.

- *the supporting questions associated with the criteria or sub-criteria - these are in italics, as in this example.*

iii.2 Summary of criteria

The hierarchy of evaluation criteria against which database management systems can be scored is summarised below and elaborated in the chapters which follow. A diagrammatic representation of the hierarchy adopted in this volume appears as Annex A. It will, of course, be necessary to construct a hierarchy applicable to the needs of any particular project or organisation, which will more than likely be a variant on the one we have illustrated.

The top level criteria are:

- Text storage - the ability of the product to organise and store the necessary volumes and types of text and other data

- Text retrieval - the capability of the product to provide a sufficient range of search, retrieval and display functions

- Text and document acquisition - the facilities for acquisition of text and other parts of documents, and to index then for subsequent retrieval

- Reports and presentation methods - support for the assembly and preparation of material from the database in report format

- Performance - the characteristics of the product in an operating environment, including performance measurement and improvement tools

- Special applications - the extent to which the product has been adapted to the needs of a group of specialised TIMS applications, office automation, records management etc

- Recent technical developments - the likelihood of the product being able to take advantage of new approaches, including special purpose hardware

- Control and security - facilities for controlling the development and use of TIMS

- Portability - the extent to which TIMS designs, data and skills are transferrable to other applications or products

- Product credibility - assessment of the credibility, experience and capability of the product and its vendor

- Application development - the extent of application development aids, including access to SSADM methods

- Project specific requirements - space for the evaluation team to include any additional requirements

- Costs - assessment of direct and ancillary costs of hardware, software, maintenance and people.

iii.3 Questions

The main body of this volume consists of a discussion of each of the above criteria together with relevant detailed questions.

The questions should be used for familiarisation with a product before attempting to allocate scores against evaluation criteria. Not all questions are relevant to all products, or projects, and they should be used selectively.

Experience has shown that little will be gained by having the vendor provide written answers to the questions. Only by probing can the evaluation team fully elicit the limits of the capabilities of the products. The best value will be obtained by attempting to answer questions after inspection of technical documentation and attending demonstrations.

Appraisal and Evaluation Library
Text-based Information Management Systems Volume

1 Text storage

1.1 General requirements

The structures and formats of Text-based Information Systems appear to be much more complex and less well defined than those which apply to more conventional numeric and coded data systems. In fact, natural language does have well defined structures - syntax and grammar - and documents are often sub-divided in practice into common-sense sections such as author, title, abstract, main text, references in journal articles; or sender, recipients, date, subject, main text in internal memoranda.

The real difficulties tend to stem from the large volumes of text involved in practical systems; the difficulty in associating meaning, or semantic values, with words which are handled as syntactic entities; the range of mutations which words of essentially the same root meaning undergo in sentence formation - plurals, tenses, gender, stress markings and so on; and the complementary problem of words of identical form with two or more meanings. These difficulties may be lessened by the use of synonym lists to related different words and phrases with similar meanings; thesauri to show the classification structures underlying subject vocabularies; and controlled language processes which filter text streams to ensure that all key terms correspond to standard versions, and sometime replace non-ideal by preferred forms. All of the aids, however complex they may become in procedures and application, form only small parts of the total storage requirement, and their consideration is deferred to Chapter 2 and 3.

Volumes

Text databases are larger, on average, than conventional DBMS by a factor of five to ten times. As a general rule, applications with 10 million characters of text (10 MB) to 50 Mb do not raise too many problems of scale; those from 50 to 250 Mb require care in design and implementation; and any from 250 Mb through the fairly common 500 Mb to the unusual 10,000 Mb (10 gigabyte, Gb) require specialist assistance, either from the vendor or from consultants practising in this field.

Variability of records   The total length of a document may vary greatly, especially in full text applications, and so do the extents of fields which subdivide the text parts. This is a significant difference from conventional DBMS where the majority of data fields are of predictable type and fixed length. In consequence, TIMS must provide efficient ways of storing variable length data from short fields like personal name, to long text extents in the case of the main body of a report. Data dictionaries, widely used for format and content control in DBMS, are much more difficult to apply to the text components.

Media   As will appear at many points in this volume, TIMS applications depend on continual and flexible interaction between the user and the database. Magnetic disc random access storage has thus become the typical medium for text databases. Magnetic tape stores are commonly used for backup. Tapes were, in the early days of TIMS development, also used in batch mode searching, and examples of magnetic tape based applications are occasionally still met. If 'digital paper' or 'digital audio tape (DAT)' should become practical, cheap, high volume, archive media - then batch searching may once more become important.

The large volumes taken up by text, and the even larger volumes of raster scanned images (see section 1.5) have lead to the use of optical disc media for TIMS applications where the database is stable and so not subject to frequent amendment. Both WORMs (Write Once, Read Many) discs and CD-ROM (Compact Disc - Read Only Memory) have been used, the latter increasingly in 'electronic publishing' applications.

1.2 Narrative forms

The earliest developments in TIMS databases followed two parallel strands, sharing similar indexing techniques. One group of products was conceived for retrieval of the full text of legal and case documents; the other concentrated on large, previously print format, bibliographic files of references to the scientific and medical literature. This FTX/ITX split is still present in much TIMS design today, and different

Chapter 1
Text storage

products, although bridging both styles, favour one or the other.

Document structures

In either case, the underlying structure is of a discontinuous stream of 'natural language' text - words, spaces, sentence marks and other punctuation, to which has been added a small range of within-document structure markers.

These may include some or all of:

- sentence dividers
- paragraph dividers
- section (otherwise 'field') labels and dividers
- fixed format 'header' zones for dates, identity numbers

Sets of documents (also 'records') may be grouped within a database into 'files' or 'sub-files' or 'chapters' to provide a subject or age related grouping of document sets.

What structural controls are provided? Do these match up to the operational requirement?

If the application involves extensive full text material, does the TIMS product provide suitable storage facilities?

Text and data

The incorporation of 'data', that is numbers, coded values and fixed format strings, within the text body of the document has been solved in several ways. The problem is to represent the data in context, but at the same time allow searching on ranges of values, especially dates; sorting; and identification of maxima and minima of values from records in retrieved subsets. One solution is to group all fields which require these facilities in a 'header zone' of fixed format fields, where they can receive special treatment. This gains in ease of implementation, and sometimes in reduced resources in updating records for data changes, at the expense of loss of the context of the data values. It is most often found in ITX applications.

A common alternative is to leave the data value in context in the text stream, but to identify it by a class marker which will permit range searching or sorting. In at least one TIMS, the actual values are stored in the pointer lists as well as in the text to facilitate handling. Context is maintained at the expense of more resource use in retrieval and updating, and with the sometimes unaesthetic effect of markers appearing in the natural flow of the text.

If tables are required in the text record, then the TIMS facilities may be strained to provide both formatted presentation and retrieval on values - it is this requirement in particular which has led designers towards the DBMS+Text solution (section 1.3).

Are tables important in the application? If so, are they stable, or is updating required?

Is retrieval on table contents required? This may include range, maximum, minimum value identification.

Does the TIMS product deal with table formats

- *within narrative structures?*

- *by gateway links to DBMS systems?*

- *by intrinsic DBMS+Text structures?*

Annotation and markup

So far the text part of the record has been assumed to be a straightforward ASCII (or EBCDIC) stream, with minimum punctuation for TIMS structure. If, however, a document has been derived from a word processor, even more so if it comes from a desktop publishing (DTP) package, then in its submitted form it is likely to contain a large set of product specific codes defining indentation, **bold** or *italic* highlights, founts and sizes, pagination, headers and footers, page ends, block protection, 'red lines' and many more.

Some TIMS products deal with this simply by stripping out all word processor related codes, and retaining only the simple form of ASCII text. This is simple, easy to implement, but often looks crude beside the original. Others do likewise, but allow both the internal (simple) form and the original (word processor form) to coexist, and they provide links so that the user may optionally see the word processor (even wysiwyg) format on screen. This gives better presentation, at the expense of duplicated storage. A variation is to index and then discard the plain text, relying always on a call to the word processor to show results screens - saving storage at the expense of more resource usage and maybe slower retrievals.

Finally, the word processor text may be retained complete, but with the markup contained as 'invisibles' within special markers. This claims to offer the best of all worlds, but is complex to implement, and is vulnerable to change in the control code vocabularies of the word processor vendors. At least one product claims to convert 'any' word processor text to a preferred format using a 'filter' package. It then operates using that format only, with an output option to translate back to the original word processor if desired. This works well so long as the 'translate' package keeps up with changes in the word processors.

Is text with word processor markup important in the operational requirement? If so, how is it provided for in the TIMS product?

Will response times suffer if storage reduction trade-offs are used in the TIMS implementation? Is there a user choice of approach?

There are few general standards applicable to TIMS packages, and little prospect that any will be agreed except for the DBMS+Text systems discussed below (section 1.3) where there is some contribution from the much more advanced standards applicable in that environment generally.

Special formats

A number of special formats may be encountered, each with its own markup conventions. They were first designed for document exchange in a specialised user community, and they have associated processors and translators for typesetting or format analysis.

- MARC (MAchine Readable Catalogue) has dialects UKMARC, USMARC, UNIMARC, AUSMARC, INDOMARK, MALMARK and many others. It is used for the exchange of bibliographic records conforming (at least in principle) to the Anglo-

American Cataloguing Rules, AACR2 1988 revision, and the transfer format is governed by the standards ISO 2709, ANSI Z39.2 and BS 4748:1982 (amended 1988). MARC has much internal sub-division of text fields by markers originally related to typesetting but now used also by special purpose retrievers, and the format is often much simplified in TIMS databases if there is no need to export records in ISO 2709 format.

- SGML (Standard Generalised Markup Language) is a format being increasingly used by publishers, where document structure is encoded by predefined markers embedded in the text. It avoids special characters except for < and > used to bound its markup codes. Apart from the appearance of these extraneous codes, it is generally easily handled in full text databases. The relevant standards are BS 6886:1987 and the equivalent ISO 8879; and the interchange format standard (DICF) BS 7138:1989 and ISO 9069.

- ODA (Office Document Architecture) is a layout based format for document exchange, as opposed to SGML, which is procedural. It is important for document transmission over PTT networks. The relevant standard is ISO 8613:1989. In principle at least, ODA documents may be expressed in SGML markup, but whether this is a practical route remains to be established outside the subject interest groups.

Are 'special' formats included in the operational requirement? If so, how are they dealt with in the TIMS product?

Are presentation or translation processors for any required special formats included in the TIMS software?

Can the use of the special format be simplified for TIMS database purposes without loss of function?

If any one of these formats is important to an application then two steps are usually important:

- Determine whether the special format must be preserved in the database, and particularly

Chapter 1
Text storage

> whether it must be available for text export. If not, then simplification of the format coding during input is often desirable.

- Refer to the standards and the recent specialised literature to determine the state of current practice, as this is an area of continuing development.

Character sets

Text-based information management systems in English language do not normally encounter character set problems, as that language (or at least its North American dialect) is a *de facto* norm for the majority of TIMS software. As soon as European languages are involved, however, extended character sets may be required, and even for cases as simple as é (e-acute) there are alternative representations.

Are European character sets required? If so, how are they accommodated in the TIMS product? Is the extended character internal representation compatible with industry standard display terminals and work-stations?

Can the database character set be simplified without significant loss of functionality? (Many diacritic marks are non-significant.)

In research papers and other technical documentation, the presence of chemical names, symbols, physical constants, logical markers and, especially, mathematical typesetting raises many problems in parsing (see section 3.3), representation in the text database, and indexing. If these character sets are present in the application requirement, then a careful study is indicated of which are retrievable, which can be carried as inactive data, and which are likely to be wholly intractable and require transcription to an easier form.

Does the TIMS product provide for extended mathematical and scientific character sets?

Can intractable text formats be transcribed, or alternatively carried as bit-mapped images within the text?

Is retrieval needed on non-standard characters?

Chinese, Japanese, Korean and some other eastern ideographic languages are well represented in the

CCCII 4-byte per character format as well as most romanised character sets. More restricted, but less space consuming formats are Digital Equipment Corporation VMS Chinese (2-byte), Wang and IBM 5550 codes. All require special terminals or workstations.

Do ideographic characters arise in the functional requirement? If so, how does the TIMS deal with them:

- *internally*

- *on screen and when printed.*

1.3   DBMS extensions

This section is concerned mainly with the text-based extensions made to DBMS products. For a general account of appraisal and evaluation of DBMS, including an introduction to the technologies involved and definitions of the various forms in use, reference should be made to the DBMS volume in this series.

From the earliest days of TIMS development there have been small scale extensions to established hierarchic and network structured DBMS products. These have generally been seen as adding to the scope of the structured DBMS, rather than as establishing text-based products *per se*, although in the last two years at least two DBMS products have shifted their emphasis towards TIMS. The advent of relational databases (R.DBMS for short) stimulated renewed interest in text retrieval as a major component of database facilities, and there are now at least as many TIMS products with this underlying structure as there are following the alternative hierarchic or network plan.

The R.DBMS+Text initiatives seem to have arisen mainly from the difficulty of dealing with tabular or volatile data within the traditional inverse file text database. The normal strategy is to declare one or more text fields (or a text 'domain') of the database to be text, and to proceed to index the contents of these fields as if they were narrative text records in themselves. Variations in treatment include 'long' fields of length up to, say, 16,000 characters stored outside the table proper; and shorter, sometimes fixed length fields kept within the table format. How the actual text is stored can vary very much, with some products generating a proliferation of sub-files and sub-sub-files for individual text extents, which simplifies implementation, but increases resource costs in access overheads during retrieval.

Apart from the immediate gain of being able to store text in text fields, and numeric or coded data in equally appropriate structured data fields, there are several advantages of the DBMS+Text approach. These include:

- Fast updating of volatile data in the non-text fields;
- Availability of data dictionary, data validation and other controls, at least on the non-text fields;
- Good facilities for recovery from system faults.

Limitations are centred on the need to use program-embedded access commands for many applications (see section 2.4).

Is a DBMS+Text approach likely to be needed for:

- *table representation and manipulation?*
- *updating of volatile, fixed format data?*
- *data validation and control?*
- *recovery from system faults?*

If so, is this structure available within the TIMS product?

The relevant international standard for relational products is the SQL (Structured Query Language) standard, ISO 9075:1989, which combines ISO 9075:1987 with the integrity addendum. Reference may also be made to BS 6964:1990 - Specification for the database language SQL. A new standard for an enhanced SQL is currently being developed (colloquially known as SQL2), and it is hoped that this upward compatible extension to the ISO 9075 language will become an international standard as soon as possible.

The corresponding international standard for network databases is the Network Data Language (NDL). CODASYL, while not producing standards, have published proposals which have influenced vendors.

Is the database schema definition language based upon an actual or proposed standard?

If so, which version of which standard and what is the degree of conformance?

To what extent is the vendor committed to making his product conform to developments of the standard?

It is necessary to identify any limits the product imposes on definition of the database structure.

Are there any significant limits applicable when defining the structure (eg number of record types, number of levels within a structure, number of fields within a record, maximum size of records etc)?

1.4 Compound documents

Documents which comprise text, complex typesetting (like mathematical functions), graphics and other diagrams, and images (like black and white photographs, or even colour) are common in practice, and have only recently moved from research into practice in text-based information management systems. The technology is not yet straightforward, and is often dependent on particular operating systems, so that solutions are not usually portable between computing platforms or application software.

The following sections deal with the main approaches which have proved to be useful in practice, roughly in order of their development and of increasing technical complexity of implementation.

TIMS calls to operating system

Many TIMS products allow the user to suspend processing and issue a system call to enter a co-existing DBMS system. This may then be used to deliver tables or perform numeric computations which are not available within the TIMS scope. Alternative uses of this sort of gateway include access to electronic mail for record acquisition or distribution; use of system editors; transfer of data files from TIMS to graphics plotters and even typesetting of search results. The main hazard is loss of context if a transient system fault occurs during operating system transfer of control, with consequent difficulty in resuming the suspended TIMS process in a tidy manner.

Does the TIMS product allow access to system services such as editors or electronic mail? If so, how is recovery from transient faults dealt with? Is text database integrity maintained if the user does not 'return' at the end of an operating system excursion?

Can operating system excursions be extended to allow DBMS operations from inside the TIMS software? If so, does this need operating system understanding, or is the user protected from this requirement?

Auxiliary devices

Gateways from TIMS can be used not only to call services within the same computer, but by transmission of suitable messages, to drive auxiliary storage units. This has been used most notably with microfilm and microfiche systems where the external retrieval is set off by a search message from the text-based system, and the desired frame is presented to the user on a separate screen.

A more technically involved procedure, but with the same basic logic, may be used to deliver high quality video-disc images from an ancillary player to a screen placed beside the TIMS terminal. This technique has been applied, for example, to clinical data systems, where high quality colour images are required to complement searching in descriptive texts. It has also been used in museum systems to present good images of material too fragile to put on display or expose to handling.

Does the TIMS allow control messages to be sent to auxiliary storage devices?

Included graphics

The next level of integration offered by a few TIMS products is to incorporate vector graphics and bit-mapped images either actually or apparently within the text part of the database. These are described as 'compound document architectures' with producer names such as CDA (Digital Equipment Corporation) and MOD:CA (International Business Machines) and others. To the user it appears as though the document contained all of the components in a continuous stream; for the system, there are choices as to whether the material is actually stored in a mixed format, or assembled 'on demand' as the text is retrieved.

Does the operational requirement include the incorporation of graphics? If so, is there flexibility between vector and bit-mapped representation?

Does the TIMS product include facilities for dealing with compound documents of the type required?

There are, for any particular application, complex design choices as to whether vector graphics and complex typesetting should be retained in its 'native' mode, revisable but requiring more software units to be currently active; or transferred to bit-mapped images which are non-revisable, consume more storage, but are simpler to handle. This is particularly a problem with storage of documents produced in office automation systems used by scientific and technical staff to write reports and papers for publication.

1.5 Storage requirements and equipment

The amount of raw text held in a TIMS system varies widely. Few working applications contain fewer than five million characters of text (5 Mb), as below this level sequential file scanning software is effective, and manual methods such as card indexes or even searching of heaps of papers are practicable. Typical indicative text (ITX) applications range from 5 Mb to 500 Mb of text, containing, for example, some 10,000 to 1,000,000 short descriptive entries, or 5,000 to 500,000 full catalogue entries respectively. Full text (FTX) systems tend to start at around 10 Mb (say 3,000 pages of office memoranda) and range up to 500 Mb, with a minority of databases taking on as much as 10,000 Mb (10 gigabytes or Gb) of accumulated text.

Text storage

The text store is not necessarily the largest file in the TIMS database, and the space overhead attributable to the indexing structures generally reduces as the text file grows. The following data are guidelines only, and should be verified for specific instances:

Indexing strategy	Overhead for small database	Overhead for large database
Inverse file	4 times text file	1.0 times text file
Inverse file, compressed	2 times text file	0.6 times text file
Signatures	0.3 times text file	0.3 times text file

The reason for the decreasing overhead ratio of inverse file databases is that the number of new words increases very much more slowly than the number of occurrences of each word after the first 2,000 terms in the vocabulary have been established. Unless deliberately unique references are indexed - such as International Standard Book Numbers (ISBN) for books - this gain in index efficiency continues indefinitely, though with decreasing marginal returns. In a fairly typical large full text database of telecommunications information (around 800 Mb) there were about 30,000 distinct words, and the five most frequent occurred between 20,000 and 50,000 times. One quarter of the words occurred five times or fewer, but many 'singles' were found to be attributable to spelling errors in the original data.

Standard signature files do not show an efficiency gain of this type, but some special algorithms for very large databases are noted in section 7.3. The use of small vocabulary signature representation, where the 'bit row' has a single position for each of about 2,000 words (or their stems) may offer indexing overheads as low as 10% for full text records such as news transcripts, but these are special cases and their application is not general.

Does the vendor of the TIMS product under assessment provide aids for calculating the volume of database storage required?

Can calculated estimates be verified by comparison with working databases of similar records and applications?

DBMS storage	The space occupied by DBMS structures is generally much less than for text databases of equivalent complexity, but is very sensitive to detailed organisation, index choice, and the use of schemas (see, for details, the DBMS volume in this series.) As a rough guide, allow for a gross storage requirement of twice the data volume to be contained in the DBMS files.
Vector graphics	Graphs, diagrams and line drawings may be concisely and effectively stored as vector graphics, that is, in the form of points, lines and polygons with text annotations. An A4 page containing a simple graph - a ten column histogram, for example - may occupy no more than 3,000 bytes of storage.

The main limitations are in the use of central processor resources to reconstruct the picture from the stored codes when it is wanted, and in the diversity of software and file formats in current use. The following format conventions are commonly encountered:

GKS	Graphical Kernel System: a portable format compatible with a range of plotting and presentation devices. This is most used in fairly large scale mathematical work.
PICT	The Macintosh internal graphics format
GDDM	The IBM mainframe internal graphics format
DDIF	The DEC internal graphics format

What exchange and storage formats are supported by the TIMS package? Do they include 'standard' versions?

What limitations of choice of terminal or work-station equipment are implied by the use of these formats?

Raster format images	Raster or bit-mapped methods represent two dimensional images by an array of black and white (sometimes colour) points in a display space. Compression algorithms are regularly used to minimise the space occupied in storage, but an A4, fairly 'busy' black and white printed page with a simple line

drawing will normally occupy 50,000 characters (bytes) after compression.

The following compression conventions are widely used, along with a number of manufacturer 'specials':

CCITT Group 3 (Equivalent to low density facsimile format)

CCITT Group 4 (Equivalent to high density facsimile format)

Scanning of images is normally at 200, 300 or 400 points per inch (78, 118 or 157 points per centimetre), and laser printers can deliver paper versions at these densities. Screen presentation is at lower resolutions, and any requirement for screen densities above 120 points per inch (47 points per centimetre) should be regarded as a special case.

The following format conventions are commonly encountered:

GDDM   The IBM mainframe internal graphics format

TIFF   Tagged Image File Format - widely used especially on IBM PC equipment and its equivalents

HPGL   The Hewlett Packard plotter format.

MacPaint The Macintosh internal image format

What exchange and storage formats are supported by the TIMS package? Do they include 'standard' versions?

What limitations of choice of terminal or work-station equipment are implied by the use of these formats?

Optical media

For large, stable TIMS applications the possibility of storage on digital optical discs in either locally writable (WORM) or mastered (CD-ROM) format is opening up new opportunities.

WORM discs appear to be cost-effective for the storage of archival TIMS data, especially when text and images are mixed. The volume at which this may be taken seriously is in the region of 2 Gb and upwards for 30 cm discs, or 100 to 150 Mb for 12 cm discs. Although the storage devices themselves are special purpose, the files stored are normally standard operating system files, and TIMS products require little adaptation for this form of mass store. There are no general standards applicable to WORM disc storage.

The CD-ROM optical disc is produced by a mastering process, and until recently has been used for text storage in published databases. The medium appears to be cost effective from 250 Mb to 600 Mb (gross) storage. Both standard and special purpose TIMS software have been used, sometimes with proprietary compression algorithms, and often requiring adaptation to deal with the relatively slow access rates characteristic of CD-ROM drives.

Standards for CD-ROM cluster around the so-called High Sierra conventions (ISO 9660), which have been effective in designating disc layouts and common directory services.

CDI extends CD-ROM capabilities to include limited numbers of image frames, sound and cartoon graphics. It is at the time of writing an immature technology, and has not yet demonstrated its information systems potential (as opposed to entertainment or educational) in practical applications. Standards are the subject of commercial differences.

2 Text retrieval

2.1 General requirements

One of the main differences between text retrieval systems and conventional DBMS is that text retrieval is inherently probabilistic and, in contrast with data retrieval, lacks absolute answers to searches. This has often been a source of misunderstanding between traditional computer departments and prospective TIMS users. In text retrieval there is a trade-off between having high recall in a search, and risking too large a results list, with many possible responses to be inspected and discarded - and looking for high precision, when all the results delivered are relevant, but some desirable records are missed because of the narrower search profiles. The achievement of both high recall and high precision is a popular target for information science research, but may in fact be not only pragmatically but also theoretically unachievable. This is a familiar topic for the information scientist, but is often found disturbing by data processing staff with a conventional computer science background, since complete recall and precision are easily obtained in data retrieval systems.

Effective TIMS systems provide, therefore, a range of aids and facilities to support the user during searching, and assist in improving the quality of results of the search. These are introduced in the remainder of this section, and a particularly important group of retrieval aids relevant to all natural language searching is described in more detail in section 2.2.

On-line

Interactive dialogue is the normal contact between the searcher and the database, with progressive refinement of queries, and development of understanding of the database content and its relation to the user's information needs. (Batch searching is, by contrast, frustrating except for the simplest, large scale runs such as producing classified listings using standardised subject fields.)

Access modes

A choice of access modes is required, allowing browsing in the database in its natural sequence of records; navigation searching based on 'known items'

Appraisal and Evaluation Library
Text-based Information Management Systems Volume

or exact keys to one document stored within another; and fully indexed searching which will retrieve on general terms within any record.

Subject and meaning   TIMS applications deal with text as a syntactic structure, that is of words and phrases, so there is no direct link between the form of the retrieved text and its meaning, until the words are read by a user. A number of aids may add subject or 'meaning' related values to the basic text. These include synonyms, thesaurus structures, stemming and truncation to remove unhelpful suffixes, and the addition of cluster or linkage markers.

Display management   Because text documents are often quite large - more than a screen of text is normal - and a retrieved set may usefully include as many as twenty or more, facilities are required for display management to make working with this material easier. Typical aids are selective displays of short sections (sometimes 'titles' or 'abstracts') from the retrieved items; showing the 'context' of keywords within the documents without listing the whole text; and allowing the user to 'zoom' from one occurrence of a search term in the text to the next rather than slowly scrolling.

Help displays   The range of commands and facilities available to the end user in a TIMS application is often large, and a context-sensitive help system is valuable both in saving time looking up the reference manuals, and in developing confidence in those new to interactive working.

The way in which text retrieval works in detail, and the facilities which are important in appraisal and evaluation form the remainder of this chapter. The potential use of artificial intelligence methods in development of user interfaces is noted in chapter 7.

2.2   **Retrieval aids**   A group of user aids, mostly to do with adding subject or meaning to the syntactic, neutral form of bare text, proves to be relevant to all of the ways of performing

Chapter 2
Text retrieval

searches, and so is discussed first. Some are relevant also to text and document acquisition, and will be referred to again in chapter 3.

Synonym structures

A synonym structure, in this context, is one which allows two or more words or phrases to be allocated the same meaning, as if they were equivalent. One may be 'preferred' in systems which exploit controlled vocabulary to simplify retrieval.

For example:

IBM
International Business Machines
Big Blue

might all be regarded as equivalent in meaning, although the first is likely to be the preferred form in a TIMS database, and the last would be expected only in news transcripts or similar informal sources. A synonym facility allows the searcher to add a control mark to the search term (for example IBM@) to mean 'that term and any declared synonyms, connected by boolean OR operators'.

Are synonyms provided in the TIMS product?

Do they include phrases as well as single words?

Can both user defined and system wide synonym sets be specified, and maintained by the end-user and the DBA respectively?

Is there a provision for preferred term marking?

Sometimes a word in English may belong to two quite separate synonym categories, for example:

lead	lead
heavy metals	manage
pollution risks	organise

In such a case the searcher must be allowed to specify which of the two or more synonym lists is desired.

Are intersecting synonym lists recognised?

Thesaurus and windows

A thesaurus extends the simple synonym relationship to allow a hierarchy of related terms to be established. This may be viewed during retrieval as a guide to likely search terms, or may be used more actively to 'expand' queries from a single simple term to include lower level categories, more general subjects or both. The usual hierarchic relationships and operators provided in a thesaurus are:

Term1 **BT** Term2	Broader term
Term1 **NT** Term2	Narrower term(s)
Term1 **USE** Term2	Term2 is preferred
Term1 **UF** Term2	Term1 is preferred (use for)
Term1 **see** Term2	Reference for indexer
Term1 **see also** Term2	Reference for indexer or user
Term1 **RT** Term2	Related term
Term1 **scope note**	Explanatory text

For example, and simplifying somewhat:

R.DBMS **BT** DBMS
R.DBMS **NT** INGRES
R.DBMS **NT** ORACLE
INQUIRE **BT** DBMS
Plex DBMS **SEE** Navigational
Data dictionary **RT** Data definition language
Optimizer **USE** Analyzer
Analyzer **UF** Optimizer

R.DBMS: **scope note** - used here for relational database management systems conforming broadly to Codd's Rules.

BT/NT, USE/UF and RT/RT come in pairs. Terms are often phrases. There is some theoretical argument as to whether a term can have more than one broader term, so forming a network rather than a simple hierarchy. For much more on thesauri see Aitchison and Gilchrist, 1987.

A simpler, sometimes complementary aid is the 'window' on the database vocabulary. This allows a searcher to enter a term or part of a term, and to see adjacent words ranked in the order used by the database.

Is a thesaurus handler included in the TIMS product?

Can an independently supplied thesaurus handler be used as an alternative? How is it interfaced?

In either case, does the thesaurus provide automatic query expansion?

Is the searcher provided with a vocabulary window?

Stemming and truncation

Words in English (and much more so in many other languages) change their form to indicate plurals, tenses and other verb forms, the person speaking, and derived nouns. For example consider:

move moves; moving; moved; remove; removes; removing; movable; moveable; removable; removable movables; removables; movement; and so on . . .

These variants may be dealt with by shortening the search word to the common stems 'mov' and 'remov' using some special character to indicate the cut-off point. If the cut is made at an arbitrary point by the searcher, it is referred to as 'truncation'. If an algorithm is used which performs the truncation by use of natural language structures at an etymologically justifiable point, it is called 'stemming'. In either case the normal practice is to remove characters from the right hand end of the word.

The effect of shortening can be to introduce ambiguity. Truncation of seats to seat* properly includes seating, seatbelt and seated. It will also find unwanted words like Seattle. Stemming is claimed to produce fewer anomalies of this sort.

Does the TIMS package provide for right truncation of words specified as terms in queries?

Is there provision for stemming?

For some applications, left-truncation is important. In English language databases, these most often occur with names of chemical compounds and pharmaceuticals, but in some languages pre-inflection for gender or case is also present. The implementation of left-truncation is generally more difficult than right truncation, involving either extra index space or recourse to sequential rather than indexed access to the word list, with corresponding loss of performance. Some special cases are dealt with in section 2.3.

Is left truncation provided?

Does this involve either space or performance penalties?

Clusters and user annotations

In some applications it is useful to be able to mark temporary or permanent clusters of documents with linkage indicators to allow them to be retrieved or browsed as a set. Examples include chains of related correspondence; references from recurrently amended statutes to later amending documents; and compilation of bibliographies for projects.

Does the TIMS software allow for chain or cluster references at database level? Are these searched only as 'retrievable' items, or are they accessible in browse mode also?

Can individual users set up cluster annotations without these being apparent to other users of the database?

These facilities are not widely available in TIMS products on the marketplace, and should be specified with caution.

Macros and command files

If a search operation is likely to be repeated a number of times, either on the same database as it changes, or on a number of compatible databases, then there are advantages to be gained from storing the search for re-use, especially if the specification is complex. There are two ways of providing this facility, somewhat overlapping in practice.

- The search may be set up as a 'command file' to be run in interactive or batch mode whenever desired.

- Alternatively, a 'macro' may be constructed which encapsulates the search requirement and also allows run-time specification of parameters such as dates, variable search terms and display layouts.

Command files tend to be simpler, but can be inflexible if the search terms are required to vary from one run to another. Macros require more investment in training and 'thinking out' when they are applied, but in some TIMS products can be made to yield a wide range of user-dedicated search aids as well as repeated query formats.

Does the TIMS product include command files for repeated searches? Across more than one database? In batch mode?

Is there a macro-processor included in the package? Can search examples be recorded and stored as potential macros?

Are either the command file or macro facilities available both at database and at individual user levels?

Ranking	A number of approaches have been developed for ranking the results of searches in an order which will assist the searcher, and some include the incorporation of user ratings of the relevance of intermediate results. Although these are promising at a research level, they are as yet uncommon in working systems, and are therefore considered in Chapter 7.
2.3 Narrative records	This section deals with retrieval in the text portion of TIMS databases. The requirements are established for text-only applications, but apply with slight modifications to the DBMS and Compound Document systems discussed in the following two sections. In this volume, no full account of the theory and practice of text retrieval is possible, and reference should be made to the books listed in Annex B for more detail.
Browsing	If a database has a 'natural' sequence, then browsing from record to record, forward, back and with jumps over 'n' records may be a useful mode of access. Examples include:

- Library catalogues in author sequence

- Bibliographic files in subject sequence

- Personnel databases in order of department and then by surname and first name

- Correspondence in order of subject, and within subject by sender, then by descending date

The user should be able to choose whether to see the whole document, in cases like catalogues or bibliographies, or a small subset - author, title, date, for example - for extended texts.

Does the TIMS product allow the insertion of new records within an existing sequence so that natural order is maintained?

Is browsing possible in this natural order?

Can the browsing user make a choice between seeing the full record or selecting a shorter subset for display?

Indexed searching

The principal form of text searching depends on the construction of **boolean search** commands. These take the basic form of a set of words (and in some products phrases), and values of date or data fields, linked by the operators AND, OR and NOT. Together with parentheses ( ) to control the sequence of processing, these may be built into the full command string. For example:

Query: 'civil servants' OR 'public employees'? finds all records which refer to either of these categories.

Query: (civil NOT 'civil servant#') AND (public NOT (('public employee#') OR ('public servant#'))? should find civil and public issues, but exclude references arising from references to people in the public service. Note the 'nesting' of subordinate parts of the query using parentheses.

The actual syntax of boolean commands varies from one vendor to another, with (at present) only the Common Command Language (CCL) and SQL offering even partial standards. If the command line format is found to be too awkward for users to deal with, and for occasional users in particular this is often the case, then a 'form-filling' or page mode retrieval may be available as an alternative, directly, or using macros. The particular form of 'query by example' is used in some products to ease the user's task of deciding how a search should be best expressed.

Is boolean query formulation in command line structure included in the TIMS product?

Does it conform to CCL, or SQL CONTAINS / CN conventions, or claim any other standard?

Are form-filling, query by example, or page mode query available as alternatives to command line syntax?

It may or may not be desirable to preserve case in indexed fields, so that 'Boolean' and 'boolean' would be separate terms.

Is case preserved in the indexing facilities?

Is the use of case distinction an on / off facility, or optional at search time?

Before launching a query, it is often desirable to check the frequencies with which the search terms appear in the database, both to limit the size of retrieved sets and to avoid excessively long searches. The facility to view the frequency of a word, or of a set of words if truncation is used, offers a valuable guide to the scale of the search. When a search, on the other hand, produces zero 'hits', an examination of the frequencies of the terms used often indicates that one of them is over-specific and should be removed.

Can the user view word frequencies in the word list?

Following a search, can the frequencies of the search terms used be examined to help to diagnose poor results?

Is there a system warning or limit to control search size

- *by looking at word frequencies?*

- *may the limit be set by the DBA?*

- *may the user over-ride the limit?*

Many text-based searches proceed in stages, with a first, fairly wide search, being followed by successive **search refinements** to narrow its scope and provide a manageable retrieved set to examine. If a search refinement step reduces the set to zero, it is important to be able to retrace at least one step, and try again. Two main alternatives are used by TIMS products:

- The software may use a so-called **sets** strategy. This forms a series of interim searches, or 'sets', storing the temporary results on a 'parking file' and finally combining two or more of the intermediate sets in a final command.

FIND civil	1 - 1,300 hits
FIND public	2 - 322 hits
COMBINE 1 AND 2	3 - 12 hits
COMBINE 1 OR 2	4 - 1557 hits
SHOW 3 FORMAT etc . . .	

- The strategy may be to find an initial set, and then reduce it in stages by **sub-queries.**

QUERY civil OR public?	1557 items
SUBQ engin* OR works?	989 items
SUBQ UK	0 items
RETRACE	989 items
SUBQ UK& (synonym)	23 items
DISPLAY etc	

The choice between these alternatives is often not technically significant. It may, however, be affected by the previous experience of library and information service staff with the commercial on-line data vendor services, most of whom, historically, have followed the 'sets' approach which reduces concurrent user contention in large networks.

Is search refinement provided?

Does it follow the strategy of

- *sets?*

- *sub-query by stages?*

Is there a way of going back one or more steps if a refinement cuts the result set to too small a scope or zero?

At the combine or sub-query stage, are intermediate results re-used to limit the processing involved, or is the whole search re-performed from the beginning given the new query constraints?

If the database has been designed to take advantage of natural document sub-divisions, or has a superimposed 'subject' related structure such as 'chapters' or 'sub-files' then the searcher may apply these **structure controls** as part of the query repertoire. The common structure controls within the query command line are:

- Groupings of records or documents

    chapter or sub-file (more or less synonymous)
    clusters or chains (see section 2.2)

- Document or record subdivisions

    document 'title'
    sections
    fields

The structure controls in wholly narrative text databases are normally simpler than those associated with DBMS+Text products, which may exploit both narrative and DBMS forms.

Does the product offer structure controls on groups of records?

What sub-record structures are available in query formation?

Are these structures also available in browsing mode?

Can the sub-record structures be used to control display also?

Those databases whose records incorporate numeric or coded values, or formatted dates, may provide corresponding retrieval tools to deal with **exact values** or **ranges** in queries. How this is performed depends on whether the fixed values are held in separate fixed format fields, or dispersed in the narrative text body (see section 1.2) but this should, if possible, not be apparent to the interactive user.

Is searching provided on 'exact matches' or 'ranges of'

- *dates (UK, US, Julian)?*
- *integer values?*
- *real values?*
- *alpha-numeric codes? (in which collate sequence?)*
- *others?*

Are the searches available (and efficient) on the whole database, or are they applicable to retrieved sub-sets only?

As well as individual words, phrases are important as access points in narrative text. In addition, it is often valuable to be able to ask for pairs or sets of words falling within a short span of each other, like *'public' within five words of 'service'*, or *'public' and 'service' in the same sentence*. These facilities are grouped under the term **proximity searching.** The term 'adjacency' is also used.

Does the vendor offer proximity searching

- *A within n words of B?*
- *A within n before, m after B?*
- *A and B in same sentence?*
- *A and B in same paragraph?*

Are phrases searchable as a special case of proximity / adjacency?

Can truncation be applied to words within a proximity search expression in a query?

If the database has been set up and indexed with word occurrence pointers down to word position within paragraphs, then proximity searching can be performed within the fixed format and efficient word lists and pointer lists. If, however, the word occurrence is addressed at record level only, then a larger set of records must be retrieved, and searched sequentially

Chapter 2
Text retrieval

for matching strings. This is normally much slower, and takes up more computer processor time.

Is proximity searching supported by word indexing?

A similar division between systems which provide facilities by indexing and those which use sequential searching is found in provision of more complex truncation and stemming facilities than are normal for TIMS software. **Left truncation** may be approached as an indexed facility by storing the word list twice, in normal and in reversed form, so that left truncated search terms become right truncated for the reversed words. This is fast and effective, but takes up disc space for extra index storage.

An alternative approach, which offers medial wild card characters also, is taken in at least one TIMS product. In this case, words in the word list are re-processed into overlapping single, two-character and three character fragments, and the fragments are hash-addressed in a **vocabulary inverted file,** carrying a pointer to the word from which they were derived. Once more, this uses disc space to gain functionality, and is exposed to occasional false drops - that is unwanted records which happen to generate the same signature as the wanted set. It does, however, provide left-, right-, and medial-truncation for those cases where it is really required. An example from chemistry would be to search for :

*but*phos*alk*

finding names like t-butylphosphaalkyne and variants with analogous forms instead of the truncation characters (*).

Is left truncation offered using direct indexing?

Can this be extended to medial elision combined with left- and right-truncation? How has this been done?

If a searcher needs to look up data from a second source while using a TIMS application, then the use of a gateway from narrative retrieval may be required. The basic resource, which leads to a range of possibilities (section 1.4) is a call to the operating system which temporarily suspends the TIMS software. This may be extended to include parameter passing to call a system editor, or to launch auxiliary database software, or processes such as electronic mail.

Does the TIMS product offer gateways from the retrieval mode to use operating system functions?

Does the range of facilities which can be accessed include

- *Operating system monitors such as time, date, resources used?*

- *System or other text editors?*

- *General purpose access to database systems?*

- *Spreadsheets or graphics packages?*

- *Electronic mail, inwards and outwards?*

- *Special purpose interfaces for compound document retrieval (see also section 2.5 below)?*

- *Others (collect details)?*

Sequential searching

In small systems, and as an auxiliary form of searching in large applications, the sequential scanning of stored text can provide useful facilities. The basic procedure is to take a 'string' of characters from the command line and match this string character by character with the text of documents in the database. If these documents are the whole database, then the working upper limit is about 5 Mb unless special hardware is used to speed up the matching (section 7.4). The search facilities provided with many word processors work on this simple basis, scanning either the documents themselves, or the document 'profiles' kept in file-and-folder structures like DEC All-in-1 and IBM PS 36.

Does the proposed TIMS product depend on sequential searching of the whole database?

If so, has special hardware been added to speed up the scanning process? (Ask for details of how it is done)

Chapter 2
Text retrieval

In larger applications, sequential searching is usually applied to sub-sets already retrieved by indexed searching to apply further criteria which the indexed approach cannot handle. These will typically include :

- Proximity searching when this cannot be done directly through the indexing facilities (see above);

- Searches involving left truncation, dual left and right truncation, and the use of internal 'wild card' characters to mean 'any one character' or 'any string of characters' in the indicated position;

- Searches which refer to special characters, that is those excluded from the indexed set because they are operators, or are reserved for other purposes (see section 3.3). Such characters often include + - / \ ( ) [ ] ' " , ; and .

Is sequential searching needed as a substitute for indexed proximity searching? If so, can its use be limited to prevent excessively long searches being launched unintentionally?

Can searches be made on truncated strings, and strings with internal wild cards?

Can sequential searching be used to identify records containing reserved characters which cannot be indexed?

The difference in performance between a simple scanning algorithm and one which takes advantage of word boundaries and its knowledge of partial matches can be significant (see, for discussions, Ashford and Willett, 1989, Chapter 12; Salton, 1989, chapter 8).

Has an improved scanning algorithm been used in the product being assessed? Which one? Is data on its method and performance published or otherwise available for assessment?

Display of results

When the searcher has retrieved a set of, say, one to twenty records believed to be of interest, display routines are used to present the text of the records on screen. The range of options, and the way in which they are applied can materially affect user satisfaction, and the overall success of a TIMS application. Commercial software products vary in the way they approach display, and practical demonstrations to groups including both systems developers and end users are recommended during assessment.

It is often found that the interaction between the structure of the text records (short or long; formatted or continuous text) and the form of presentation (form-like; page by page; text streams in windows) is sensitive, and small changes can significantly affect user acceptance. These preferences may later change with experience of use in practice, placing a premium on flexibility in the TIMS software for display management.

The first step in reviewing a retrieved set is often to browse rapidly through a short portion of each record. This may be a built-in facility to show a record 'title' or 'abstract' section, or may require a short display format to be prepared. Records which are identified from the short entry as being of interest may then be displayed in full.

Is there a standard form of short display?

Is there an alternative way of building up a short display using the general display formatting software?

Formatting of the displays more generally depends on a number of facilities. It is reasonable to expect :

- selection of designated sections or fields of the record, and ordering in a presentation sequence different from that stored in the database;

- sorting of the retrieved set on specified fields or embedded values prior to display;

- layout of tables embedded in the text, including reasonable wrap-round when the table span exceeds the screen width;

- an option to highlight search terms (on suitable screens) to alert the user to their position in the text.

The variable length format of many documents causes difficulties in screen presentation, and may involve compromises in application design for both short and long fields. The options which may be expected in TIMS software include - not all in every package :

- structured, form-like presentation of short records with many fields (for example, bibliographic data);

- page by page display, often with adjustable indentation, of continuous texts with little or no formal structure (committee minutes, interview transcripts);

- structured display with 'windows' within which variable length text may be scrolled (statutes; technical reports in standard formats; accident / incident reports).

It is also useful to have the option to display the search history during display as well as during searching, as examination of the retrieved records often raises questions about the way in which the selection was performed, and leads to re-selection or additions to the retrieved set based on new concepts.

What display facilities are provided for

- *selection of document subsets?*

- *sorting of retrieved records?*

- *layout of tables?*

- *highlighting of search terms?*

- *structured record display? with scrollable windows?*

- *page by page display?*

In longer bodies of text, especially when several retrieved records are expected to be of interest, it is tedious to have to page up and down looking for passages of interest. A simple aid is to be able to highlight the words on which searching was done where they occur in the text. More effective, especially in multiple records is a 'context' command which will display, for every search term, the line containing the term, the line before and the line after. For long, unstructured texts, a 'zoom' facility allows skipping forward to the page containing the next occurrence of a search term, or alternatively, the next occurrence of a new string of characters.

Does the TIMS software provide for easy movements in long texts through:

- *a context command?*

- *a zoom command?*

Note that the term 'zoom' has been used in somewhat different senses at various times by on-line database vendors.

Transfers to files

If the results of a search are to be listed, or to be further processed, for example in a word processor for improved presentation or incorporation in a report, or by a report writing package, it is necessary to transfer the retrieved set to a system file. For transfers to other TIMS databases, the internal markup is required, but for other applications the 'presentation' form of the document may be all that is required. In either case a transfer command is needed, or a routing option within the existing display repertoire, to move the retrieved records, or selected sections to a designated file.

Can retrieved records be routed to a named system file?

Are there facilities to select particular sections for transfer?

What options are available to transfer internal markup, or add annotation to the records written to file?

Sometimes it is convenient to store parts of texts temporarily in work files, especially if sections from various sources are to be compared, or calculation done on tabular data.

Does the TIMS software include dedicated work files accessible to the end-user?

Are these work files for the current session only (deleted on log-off) or can the user carry them on to a future session?

Chapter 2
Text retrieval

Differences in signature based systems

The preceding discussion has been centred on the most widely used, traditional inverse file TIMS systems. Signature based systems, which save on space used for indexes, and sometimes on update and insertion processing costs, are more limited in the search and display facilities which they can provide. The main differences are noted below.

- Synonyms and thesaurus entries are more difficult to handle in signature systems, especially when phrases are involved. If they are provided, it is desirable to check on the method of implementation, and to try to establish any inherent limitations. Refer also to truncation and stemming;

- Since there is no word list as such, windows on the vocabulary and frequency counts are unlikely to be provided;

- Truncation is inherently difficult because each word is hash indexed as a unit, and truncated search may be possible only by sequential scanning of the text body. Stemming is more practical, but only as a choice between 'always on' and 'always off' as the decision is required prior to building up the signature arrays;

- Proximity searching is always difficult to provide, and usually depends on scanning of the texts of a set of records selected on the separate words used in the query. Some products allow phrases or pairs of adjacent words to be indexed as well as individual words.

Display facilities are not further limited by the indexing strategy and are usually comparable to inverted file products.

If the TIMS uses signature indexing, does it incorporate functions to provide

- *controlled language (such as a thesaurus)?*

- *stemming as an alternative to truncation?*

- *limits on long searches?*

- *searching on phrases or words in proximity?*

2.4 DBMS based systems   So far as the narrative text retrieval in a DBMS+Text application is concerned, the majority of the features discussed in sections 2.2 and 2.3 above may be expected at some level of implementation. The main differences arise from the much richer provision in DBMS of functions related to data fields and tables, so that those parts of narrative text which might have served these purposes are replaced by the corresponding parts of the DBMS. Retrieval on the non-text parts of a DBMS+Text record is standard, and reference should be made to *Appraisal and Evaluation of Database Management Systems* in this series. So far as text is concerned, there appears to be little practical difference between hierarchic or network products and the relational database systems, although details of the command language differ.

Language extensions   The general form of language extension is to introduce into the standard database query format an extra reserved word. In relational DBMS implementations using SQL this has often taken the form of CONTAINS or CN within the WHERE clause. This is interpreted to treat the remainder of the WHERE clause as text-directed retrieval criteria applied to the column whose name lies between the WHERE and the CONTAINS. The syntax within the CONTAINS section usually follows that described for narrative text TIMS fairly closely.

Chapter 2
Text retrieval

Example from a maps catalogue (Ashford and Willett, 1989)

```
SELECT MAPID,NAME,SCALE,TYPE,DATE
FROM UKCS
WHERE SCALE < 1,000,000
AND SCALE ≥ 50,000
AND TYPE CN(('SOLID' OR 'SUBSUR*') NOT 'DRIFT')
AND COUNTRY CN ('UK&' OR 'NORWAY')
AND NAME CN (('VIKING' OR 'CEN*') AND 'GRABEN')
ORDER BY NWY,NWX;
```

Text searching is typically interactive, and there are two ways in which this can be achieved in DBMS+Text products. The first is to embed the SQL or other query statements in an application program which communicates with the user through a program defined interface. Query terms and operators are assembled by the application program from the user interactions, loaded into the database query, and executed. This approach can be used to deliver well adapted and customised applications, with user interfaces more or less consistent across text and data aspects of retrieval. It also makes it easier to specify format for displays and dealing with recovery from system failures or interruptions. On the other hand, design and implementation times and costs are high, and the result may be a relatively inflexible solution.

The alternative is to use a free standing variant of the database to simulate the behaviour of the traditional narrative text TIMS, and allow the user to direct the form and progress of retrieval. This meets the need for interactive dialogue and for flexibility, but the interface may be unduly simple or unhelpful, and DBMS recovery and monitoring services may not be fully exploited. In an ideal DBMS+Text TIMS, both approaches are available.

Is the search language

- *program embedded?*
- *free-standing?*
- *available in both modes?*

Appraisal and Evaluation Library
Text-based Information Management Systems Volume

Has advantage been taken of 'screen painting' or other interface utilities in the DBMS to provide adaptable search interfaces?

Integration

The following functions are normally best expressed in the text part or the DBMS part of the hybrid TIMS, and the overall design is required to handle the integration of the two with a minimum of user intervention:

Text part	**DBMS**
Narrative text	Data and coded fields
Truncation	Range search
Proximity search	Validation
Highlighting	Tables
Context and zoom	Computation

Has the vendor provided a smooth integration between the text-based and the structure-based components of the DBMS+Text TIMS software?

Has advantage been taken of FORMS or other interface utilities in the DBMS to provide adaptable display interfaces?

2.5 Compound documents

The development of standard, packaged approaches for materials in compound document architecture (CDA) is, at the time of writing, still very much in progress, and it is not yet clear which standards or approaches will become established. Some vendors are proposing to attach their products to the DEC CDA and / or the IBM MO:DCA protocols. Others believe that is it as yet more effective, both functionally and in cost terms, to solve each case on its merits, taking advantage of a developing library of procedures and interfaces to do so.

Does the TIMS deal with compound document architectures

- *at all?*

- *using manufacturers' standard operating system tools?*

- *as an ad hoc requirement using established libraries?*

Chapter 2
Text retrieval

The following sections provide a provisional approach to the key features of assessment of development proposals, but should be expected to change. Specific criteria will be added in future editions of this volume as more practical experience is gained on a much wider range of projects than is available at present.

Retrieval language

The form and scope of the retrieval language are subject to the criteria developed above for narrative and DBMS-based products. In addition the following facilities are required:

- references or pointers in the text, or in suitable data fields to link up to vector graphics or image files. If these files are interleaved with the text of the document, the linkage is simplified, but the problems of storage increase;

- graphics quality screen to show images as they are retrieved or context sensitive filters to suppress images on terminals or workstations not equipped to display them. This process may become quite complex if the software sets out to identify the terminal and adapt the whole presentation accordingly - as has been partly achieved with some geographic information systems (GIS);

- window presentation where appropriate, to allow parallel viewing of text and images. This is particularly important if personal computers with relatively small screen areas are used as the workstations;

- document assembly for 'export'. A common application of TIMS is to search out material from a number of documents, compile a single report and transmit this by electronic mail to its requestor. For compound documents, the TIMS facilities must be matched by corresponding compound document capabilities in the editor, and in the electronic mail system in use.

How does the TIMS incorporate references to graphics or images

- *by embedding binary files in the text?*

- *by a pointer reference structure?*

Are graphics screens included?

Can text and graphics be viewed side-by-side in a 'window' or similar format?

How are compound documents assembled for file transfer?

Does the text editor incorporate suitable extensions for dealing with vector and image components?

Network load

Bit-mapped images take up large volumes of storage (Chapter 1) and are often placed on dedicated magnetic disc or optical disc units. In planning compound document management systems, it is necessary to consider the load placed on any communications networks involved, as this may increase sharply when images are introduced.

A substantial report, say 20 pages of A4 text produced on a word processor, may amount to 50,000 characters of text and result in the transmission of 75,000 bytes of information if it is retrieved over a network. If five of the twenty pages are replaced by compressed images of scanned drawings, the volume transmitted increases by a factor of four or more, and a line occupancy of one-third seconds at 10 Mhz is introduced. This is not significant for a single user, but may rapidly build up a potentially critical load on an already busy network if several users are concurrently active on the TIMS. If images are handled in uncompressed form, then a further five-fold increase in volume transmitted may be expected.

Does the TIMS compress images in raster format?

If so, what format is used?

What are the implications for network load for the application being considered?

3 Text and document acquisition

Except for those text-based information systems which make a new start and build a database from the beginning, the retrospective conversion of existing records to computer readable format is likely to be a major expense and a focus for problems in setting up the application. Even where no existing records are to be acquired, the requirements for text acquisition are frequently underestimated, and lead to extra and unforseen costs in developing auxiliary software for interface modules.

Record formats and mark-up conventions have been discussed in Chapter 1, and these aspects are referred to only briefly here.

3.1 Sources on paper

Small volumes of text for retrospective conversion, and small volume updates to existing databases are often best re-keyed, rather than setting up and testing automated routines. As a guide to transcription costs, the keying, proofreading and quality checking of text taken from clean originals yields between 5 and 10 Mb of converted text per person-year. Where within this range a particular project will fall depends on keyboard skills, management and motivation, and the inherent complexity of the records to be transcribed. For some applications it may be desirable to capture the text using a word processing or simple data entry system, and then convert to TIMS format separately.

What text and data entry facilities are provided for the original keying of database content

- *for long texts?*

- *for structured texts?*

- *for mixed text and data?*

Is data validation provided?

Can text fields be matched with thesaurus or other controlled vocabulary aids during input? or in batch mode later?

What facilities are available for proofreading of new texts, and the correction of transcription and other errors?

Are facilities available for operator performance measurement?

Transcription projects of more than 300 Mb have been successfully carried out, especially on bibliographic records. These projects have a history of struggles to maintain accuracy in the converted data.

The alternative for text, and the only realistic method for graphics and images, is to use some form of automated, or at least computer assisted transcription. Voice recognition for direct transcription is promising, but few practical applications are reported.

Text and data

The normal path for automated text acquisition from paper is through optical character recognition systems. These have recently become much cheaper, and are typically micro-computer driven. If a large OCR based conversion is proposed, this should be the subject of a specific functional requirement analysis, as the form of OCR required is usually sensitive to founts, paper size and quality, binding and similar physical constraints.

For the TIMS product, questions concern interfacing.

Is there a transfer interface for the proposed OCR server to the TIMS package in question?

Does the OCR scanner software insert structure markers for TIMS text input? If so, which TIMS products are included?

It is important to define the error rates that are to be expected, and what action is required for corrections.

Does the TIMS software provide for detection of transcription errors

- *in control or structure fields?*

- *in text or data fields?*

How are these edited to make corrections?

Graphics and images

Material in these categories must normally either be redrawn using computer-based draughting software or, more often, scanned as a raster image. Transfer formats should be considered when selecting the scanning device.

What transfer file formats does the TIMS support?

3.2 Sources in computers

If the sources of material for the TIMS database are already in computer readable format, then the conversion tasks - and costs - are usually much reduced.

Text and data

Typical sources are office automation systems - especially word processing, typesetting files and news or conference transcripts. For bibliographic records, and for a rapidly growing range of other materials including patents and standards, text sources are available on CD-ROM and licenses to 'down-load' text may be obtained.

What transfer file formats does the TIMS support?

Does the source insert structure markers for TIMS text input? If not, how is it to be inserted?

Is word processor or desktop publishing mark-up

- *retained and concealed?*
- *stripped out?*
- *replaced by alternative mark-up special to the TIMS package?*

Graphics and images

These are likely to be application special. Sources may include computer aided draughting packages; business graphics; data logging and analysis software; chemical structure handlers; general mathematical and statistical plotting aids; 'paint' software; desktop publishing; scanned image stores; digitised photographic or video images; satellite images; radar plots and many others. Many have specialised formats.

What transfer file formats does the TIMS support?

Does the source insert structure markers for TIMS text input? If not, how is it to be inserted?

3.3 Parsing requirements

Under 'parsing' are included all the processes necessary to convert raw text to an indexable and retrievable form in the TIMS database. For details see the references in Annex B.

Structure

The parser must be able to identify the way in which the incoming text fits into the database record structure. This may be done entirely by markers embedded in the text, or may depend on the screen formatting used in the entry interface.

How is the record structure indicated to the parser?

Are default or error correction routines provided to deal with minor errors in structure?

How does the parser recognise input text to be inserted in specific locations in the database to maintain 'natural sequence' as described in section 2.3?

Indexing

It is important to be able to define, within the text record structure, components to be indexed. This applies to fields, words, characters and the handling of long text spans.

What facilities are made for selective indexing at field level

- *include or exclude field?*

- *treat as text or data value or date?*

- *treat as controlled vocabulary (see also below)?*

Can 'stop words' be defined, not-to-be-indexed wherever they occur in text? If so, can new stop words be marked in the database retrospectively?

Can a word which has been a stop word be made active for indexing? If so, at what cost?

How is the indexable character set defined?

Chapter 3
Text and document acquisition

Is there an option to preserve 'case' in indexable items? Is there then an option to recognise acronyms (all caps.) separately?

Is there a user option to add or remove characters from the indexable set?

Many 'new' words in the index turn out to be spelling errors. These are more readily removed if the parser lists all new occurrences as the text is matched with the word list during processing.

Is there provision for a 'new words' listing?

Vocabulary control

The principles behind vocabulary control, and the general appraisal criteria are discussed in section 2.2. In the parsing stage the following requirements may be identified.

Is there provision for selection of controlled words and phrases

- *in designated sections? (maybe called 'keywords')*
- *marked in the body of the text?*

Is control applied during parsing? with options of

- *automatic substitution of preferred terms?*
- *interactive annotation or editing?*

There is a particular vocabulary problem when a phrase made up of two or three words occurs moderately frequently, and is a useful access point, whereas each word by itself occurs often so that proximity searching becomes slow. Examples include 'North Sea', 'structural steel', 'High Street' and 'ion density' in different contexts. One solution is to allow phrases to be 'bound' by a character like underscore, which turns them into separate entities. Others use angle brackets < > or special quotes for this purpose.

Is there provision for phrase binding?

Stemming

In those systems which offer 'stemming' as a retrieval aid, this must normally be set up as the text is acquired and indexed prior to updating. For these systems

Are the stemming algorithms documented?

Can the user make alterations to rules or procedures to suit particular applications or local vocabularies?

Is stemming an on/off option, or can both stemmed and non-stemmed word forms be indexed and searched?

Signature systems

These products generally have fewer options on data structure and retrieval aids than the traditional inverse file TIMS, and the text acquisition requirements are correspondingly simpler. Each product is likely to have its own particular approach to storage and indexing. This should be investigated and documented, so that the range of input facilities can be checked against the way in which the data will be retrieved.

There are few general rules for what to expect in signature based TIMS, and many commercial products will be found to be closely bound to a particular word processor or other text source.

3.4 TIMS maintenance

Almost all TIMS databases change over time by adding records, and most must provide for amendment of existing text and data.

Text changes

When changes are made to the text of a record, both the stored text and the indexes must be updated. This may use a TIMS specific editor, or, more usually, allow access to a system editor to make the changes. Records may be updated immediately ('on-line'), or kept for a batch update of the revisions later.

What provisions are made for editing existing text?

If the update of the indexes is deferred, is the record marked in some way to indicate to users that a change is pending?

Can the amended record be viewed by a searcher?

Chapter 3
Text and document acquisition

Can successive amendments be made to the same record without loss of control of the sequence of actions?

Revisable data

If data is embedded in narrative text, the amendment processes are similar to those for text proper and the use of deferred updating is also common. In those cases where the data elements are held in fixed fields in a mainly narrative text database, then updating of each field may be easier.

How are data elements updated?

DBMS changes

In DBMS+Text systems, changes to text are normally handled as in the narrative text TIMS, and changes to data follow the rules for structured or relational databases (see Appraisal and Evaluation of Database Management Systems in this series).

What provisions are made for editing existing text?

What provisions are made for editing existing data?

If the update of the indexes is deferred, is the record marked in some way to indicate to users that a change is pending to either text or data?

Can the amended record be viewed by a searcher?

Can successive amendments be made to the same record without loss of control of the sequence of actions?

Graphics and images

There appear, at least in current TIMS products, to be few options for graphics and images except deletion of an existing item and its link from the text record, and replacement by a new image and a new link. Each product should be examined on its merits, taking account of:

- ease of making the changes

- robustness to user errors

- provisions for recovery from system failures while the changes are in process.

How easy is it to make changes to graphics and images?

Is the user protected from errors in procedure or syntax?

Does system recovery deal with failures during update of graphics or images?

On-line updating

Updating of the text files and especially of the word lists and pointer sets is a complex task for inverse file products. Some of them - especially R.DBMS+Text - choose to re-index a field or section completely, in batch mode, if one or more changes are made. Signature files can usually add new records much more easily than making changes to index rows for existing texts.

For those few TIMS applications which require immediate updating of changes, this causes difficulties. The update of even small numbers of records in batch is usually too time-consuming to be acceptable, and locks up the database for searchers while it takes place. Real on-line updating which does not interrupt the use of the database is difficult to implement and heavy on central processor and disc channel resources.

Is the on-line update really required by the application?

Does the TIMS product being assessed have facilities for on-line updating, including recovery if system failures occur during changes to the word list and pointer files?

What is the resource cost of on-line updating compared with deferred updates in batch mode?

The relatively few published applications where on-line updating has been justified and successfully implemented include police authority incident reporting and investigation systems; monitoring of computing and communications networks including 'help desk' records; and transcripts of legislative assemblies.

Weeding

Many TIMS accrue quantities of out-of-date or redundant records. It are usually desirable to remove this material by some sort of 'weeding' process, based on retrieving and deleting the unwanted material. Deletes in a TIMS database are often heavy on resources as all references to all words in the deleted document must be traced and eliminated, and few of the short-cuts which can be used in the insertion task can be made to work when deleting.

One option is not to delete, but to mark records so that they disappear for the user. This saves update resources, but leads to cluttered indexes, wasted text file space, and gradual loss of retrieval efficiency as more and more records are retrieved, and then found to be condemned.

Does the TIMS genuinely delete unwanted records?

If records in the database can be grouped into sub-files by date or by subject, then some TIMS provide more efficient facilities for block deletion of these segments.

Is block deletion of unwanted records available?

Appraisal and Evaluation Library
Text-based Information Management Systems Volume

4 Reports and presentation methods

Although the main applications of text-based information systems are normally on-line, and the valuable interactive processes of query refinement and user assessment of retrieved material are missing in batch processes, the use of report writers and other software to produce large or periodic outputs is not uncommon.

In the early days of text retrieval (say 1968 - 73) most output was from batch runs, and the problems of receiving either vast heaps of printout or none were a deterrent. The approaches developed at that time to achieve control are still visible, especially in the online bibliographic systems. They include the use of strictly controlled keyword or index fields, limitation of free text fields to a few lines, and sorting on short, fixed format key items.

It should be recognised during the feasibility study stage of a project, that the generation of printed output from a TIMS database, especially in a form suitable for publication, may cause many apparently trivial but tedious problems in implementation, and take a disproportionate amount of time to bring to a satisfactory state. Short, formatted text records, and informal long free text output both appear to cause less trouble. Mixtures of text and tables, and the production of page formatted, sorted reports with headers and footers, are most difficult.

4.1 Report writers

When a TIMS in the form of a DBMS+Text (section 2.4) is used, or if a standard report writer can accept files transferred from a narrative TIMS product, then some classes of report become straightforward. For DBMS+Text the data extraction and transfer should be intrinsic and straightforward.

When a narrative TIMS is used as the source for a standard report writer, the transfer of material from one to the other may require attention, especially to intermediate record formats.

Does the TIMS software provide for file transfer of search results (as in section 2.3, Transfers to files)?

Does the proposed Report Writer accept transfer files in the format generated by the TIMS software, or is an intermediate formatting programme necessary?

Are the character sets compatible across a TIMS application and an independent Report Writer package?

The use of one or other of these routes to report production (called hereafter the 'report writer' route for simplicity) involves the following considerations:

- The production of reports normally involves sorting of the contents into at least one sequence. If the sort keys can be derived from fixed length numeric or coded fields, this is usually easy. With text fields, however, problems arise of variable length, and, more seriously, of key generation. Personal names and conventional subject codes cause some of the more involved problems, for example:

A B Smith	Arnold Smith
A. B. Smith	Arnold B Smith
Dr A B Smith	Prof. A B Smith
Dean Smith	Dean A B Smith
A Brown-Smith	Arnold Brown-Smith

    669.14: 621.785 (annealing; steel)
    669.71: 621.785 (annealing; aluminium)
    669.3: 621.785 (annealing; copper)
    643.352.3: 669.71 (aluminium; saucepans)
    643.352.3: 669.3 (copper; saucepans)

    There are well established rules for dealing with the sequencing of these, and other arbitrary or 'canonical' sequences (Works of Shakespeare; Books of the Bible, Acts of Parliament, etc) but these are unlikely to be represented in general purpose Report Writers. The use of an application specific program to convert awkward keys into more easily sortable formats is common.

- The production of report sections based on formatted fields is normally straightforward and well within the scope of standard software.

Chapter 4
Reports and presentation methods

- It may be required to produce derived tables with computed values, groupings, and totals, based on the data transferred to the Report Writer. This is also usually straightforward, but for complex requirements reference should also be made to the volumes in this series on application generators and DBMS.

- The handling of variable length, and especially longer text elements can be troublesome in Report Writers, especially when text must be 'wrapped' from one line to the next using a different line length from the source. All sorts of layout problems arise, especially at page breaks, and if this functionality is important, demonstration by vendors on realistic data samples are usually necessary.

The following questions arise during appraisal:

Are 'multiple' sorts required - title within subject or title within author for example?

Is sorting involved on variable length or complex text fields? If so, is this supported by the Report Writer?

Is sorting involved which requires canonical sequences? If so, are extra - special purpose - programs required to generate auxiliary sort keys?

Does the Report Writer handle variable length text fields which occupy:

- *less than one line?*
- *a few lines?*
- *many lines?*

Can header and footer contents be derived from the text fields during report pagination?

Is double or multiple column formatting within pages supported for reports of short structured records like catalogue entries?

4.2 Indexes

Index applications rely on the TIMS database as a source for published indexes of one form or another.

They include current awareness bulletins and subject information bulletins (based on bibliographic records); briefings and updates (based on topic extracts from news transcript sources); and print-format documentation sets for permanent record purposes (health and safety records; pharmaceutical adverse reaction data; analyses of 'help desk' responses).

Some TIMS products provide a wide range of controlled language and other formal indexing aids (see section 2.2). They then apply these indexing aids in the production of formatted bulletins and other reports, adding features such as cross-references, active data entered in page headings, subject section headings and others. Most TIMS extensions of this type were developed for special library purposes, are in well established styles of presentation, and may prove inflexible for wider applications. If, however, the production of, for example, current awareness bulletins, is a main application requirement, then such ancillary software may affect the choice of a TIMS product.

Is there a strong application requirement for traditional index or subject bulletin production? If so,

Is the TIMS/Report Writer alternative reasonably suited to this requirement? Otherwise,

. . . . consider an appraisal restriction based on the scope of the report or index production functions of the TIMS products under consideration.

4.3 OA and DTP systems

A much more flexible alternative, and one which is becoming more and more widely used, is to exploit the TIMS facilities for database management and searching, but to assign the subsequent presentation tasks to advanced word processing (OA) or desktop publishing (DTP) products.

Small selections are usually easy. If there is any form of transfer of retrieved results to file, then the results can usually be loaded directly into a word processor for editing and document production. Since the volumes are small, there is little concern over the amount of intervention needed in the preparation, and the method is extremely flexible. It is for the larger

Chapter 4
Reports and presentation methods

volumes of retrieved material - say 100 records or 20,000 characters of text upwards - that automation of the transfer and formatting procedures is worth while.

Sorting of the retrieved records is once more likely to be a serious consideration. If the TIMS database supports 'natural sequence' (section 2.3) and this is also the desirable sequence for reports, then the sort problems may be side-stepped.

Transfer formats depend very much on the strategy adopted for text acquisition and integration with OA generally (sections 3.2 and 6.1). If OA markup is preserved in the TIMS, then the transfer files should be directly usable, but sorting may need more care if special characters are interpolated in the visible text. (Consider the correct sequence for 'types', **types** and *types*.)

Once the selected records have been transferred, the processing can be very flexible, and a rich range of functions is available in most commercial DTP products. If a run is to be repeated with little change from time to time, then the availability of 'macros' or other means of preserving formatting steps may be of value.

Can sorting be avoided using 'natural sequence' in the TIMS database? (See implications for updating, section 2.3 - browsing)

Is sorting involved which requires canonical sequences? If so, are extra - special purpose - programs required to generate auxiliary sort keys?

Is OA markup preserved in the TIMS so that transferred text is directly usable for OA/DTP processing? If not, how is OA markup to be restored?

If some of the TIMS being considered restrict the range of OA/DTP products which can be applied, it may be necessary to make a subsidiary study of the processing scope required at this stage to assess whether this is a limitation on product choice for the TIMS itself. At least in the Macintosh environment, and probably soon in the IBM PC domain also, exchange between formats of different word processing products may be looked for. The exchange process (also called 'filtering') is, however, prone to unpredictable minor failures for uncommon conditions, and re-proofing may be required.

The production of this manual, for instance, involved exchange of word processing files among the MSDOS versions 4.2, 5.0 and 5.1 of WordPerfect, and versions 1.0.1 and 1.0.5 of the same package on the Macintosh IIcx. Only the earlier Mac version failed to make at least a reasonable conversion, and the latest versions on each operating system lost very little format information and no text.

5 Performance

For all except the smallest TIMS applications, the performance of the system is an important consideration for the designer. Since text based applications tend naturally to large storage volumes, the time and resources taken up in storage and updating of TIMS databases, and (less often) in searching can be important. Benchmarking has often been found desirable in final selection between similar competing products, and provided that care is taken to ensure text data sets which are representative both in content and scale, this can be a valuable approach. The availability of performance measurement and 'tuning' tools and other utility programs may also be an aspect of product selection.

5.1 Serviceability

Serviceability relates to the ability of the TIMS to provide suitable service, to maintain the integrity of the data, and, in particular, be resilient to hardware or software malfunction.

Most of this section is concerned with the text aspects of TIMS databases. For a more extended account of DBMS requirements, see *Appraisal & Evaluation of Database Management Systems* in this series.

Multi user functions

It is important that the TIMS adequately supports suitable levels of concurrent usage and ensures that there are no problems arising from data contention. The number of users that a TIMS can support may be limited by any one of a number of factors, including commercial restrictions, available memory, operating system limitations and the design of the TIMS software itself.

Is there a limit on the number of concurrent users

- *entitled to search and read the database only?*
- *entitled to add or modify data?*

What are the limiting factors and how do they affect the maximum?

It is important to establish the memory resources required. In a shared service environment many factors must be considered - the total number of logged on users; the proportion concurrently active; the temporary work space required for retrieved set manipulation; and, in some operating systems, 'locked pages' to limit storage exchange to disc. There is always at least the basic memory requirement for the system and TIMS software nucleus plus individual storage requirements for each user. Storage for buffers and work space may be variable, but a realistic minimum amount is required.

What is the main storage requirement for the TIMS:

- *on-line applications?*

- *batch applications?*

Can the TIMS support shared (update) access to data by on-line application programs? . . . and by batch application programs while there are interactive searchers?

Products can run out of memory when more than a handful of users try to access the system, so techniques such as multi-threading are often used.

Is there a recommended minimum amount of machine resource that should be allowed for each concurrent user?

Recovery

On-line updating of data in a multi-user environment requires that the mechanisms within the TIMS provide the ability to recover from any form of failure. This normally requires that log files have to be used to keep a record of all actions that have changed the data.

Recovery may be addressed from two viewpoints:

- the mechanisms available in the product for backup and restore, logging, and rollback;

- how the product deals with a specific form of failure; of the application, media, etc.

Criteria are provided below for the first - mechanisms - viewpoint, which is normally more effective for TIMS

Chapter 5
Performance

assessment. In an evaluation this should be chosen for weighting and scoring - the other may then be used to gain further insights into the capability of the products. Note that in general the recovery features of TIMS systems are less well developed than for standard DBMS, and that many assume batch rather than immediate recovery of system failures.

Backup and restore

Dumping the whole database produces a self consistent copy, but may not be practical for large databases. If selected parts only are dumped, care must be taken to ensure that dumped and undumped parts are restored to a common consistent state.

What forms of database dumping are allowed:

- *whole database?*

- *selected parts of the database?*

Database backups may either be taken as an image of the disk, or a backup of the data files. The former is usually quicker, but offers less control when carrying out a restore.

What types of database archive can be taken:

- *image dump?*

- *data backup?*

Systems requiring constant availability may necessitate dumping part of the database while applications are still processing it. This means that the dumped portion is not necessarily self consistent. When restored, the update transaction journal must be processed to roll forward those records changed between the time they were dumped and the end of the dumping operation. (This feature is more likely to be found in DBMS+Text systems.)

Can the database be dumped while applications are active? If so, how is consistency maintained?

In DBMS+Text systems especially, updates to volatile data are likely to cause many entries in the log. For

83

recovery purposes, only the most recent entry may be relevant. It is useful to have a utility that deletes all except the most recent entry and also minimises head movement time during reprocessing.

Are utilities available to compress or reorder log information for efficient reprocessing when restoring and rolling forward a database?

Logs

In order to return the database to a consistent up to date state following failure and restoration of the backup it is essential to have 'logs' (or journals) available to 'roll forward' the database.

What form of logs are held to enable database roll forward:

- *transaction logs? (Usual in TIMS)*

- *after image logs? (Mainly in DBMS+Text systems)*

Some systems require specific device types (eg tapes) for logging.

What device types are required for logs and journals?

Rollback

The TIMS must have a strategy for removing, or 'rolling back', the effects of incorrect or incomplete transactions. For search transactions this is usually straightforward if loss of the current interactive query is accepted by the user - a common approach. Online updating is more complex, and rollback is usually accomplished either by recording the state of the data before update, that is 'before images', or by not physically writing any data until the transaction has been successfully completed.

What strategy is used for ensuring that incomplete or incorrect transactions can be rolled back?

Authority

It may be a requirement that database level recovery be initiated only by persons with 'database administrator' authority. DBMS+Text applications should be able to roll back their own updates to the last (application defined) checkpoint.

Chapter 5
Performance

What level of database recovery can be initiated:

- *by an application?*

- *by other means (please specify)?*

What controls are applied to prevent unauthorised initiation of recovery procedures?

Media failure

If database media failure is discovered when reading or writing data it may be possible to circumvent the damaged media or the database may have to be stopped and a recovery instigated.

What happens if the TIMS discovers a media failure? Is the intervention of an operator called for?

Failure of the logging media is often not detected until it is required in a recovery. The only safeguards are to run duplex logs, or to make backup copies of all logs. (Do not expect too much in TIMS software.)

Are any utilities available to overcome corruption of the logging media?

System failure

Processor or system software failure usually means that the TIMS loses control, with the database being left in an indeterminate state. Full recovery from an established restart point will be required.

How does the TIMS recover from a processor or system software failure?

Resilience

If uninterrupted operation is important, then duplexing of data and journals as an insurance against media failure may be important. (This is not a common requirement in TIMS applications; when it does occur it requires special attention as this is an area where TIMS software tends to be weak.)

Does the TIMS provide for duplexing of data, text and journals?

Data integrity
The term integrity is used in database contexts with the meaning of accuracy, correctness, or validity. The object is to guard the database against invalid updates. Invalid updates can be caused by errors in data entry, by mistakes on the part of the operator or the application program, or by system failure. A database is said to be in a consistent state when all items in the database that should be in agreement with or compatible with each other are in such a state.

Data integrity is maintained both by ensuring that the data is in a consistent state as input, but also by ensuring that such input complies with restraints defined in the specification. Some R.DBMS systems include the ability to define integrity constraints that will be validated automatically. Such features are considered by many data processing professionals to be essential in a shared data environment as applications cannot be trusted to maintain the data integrity of the database. However such facilities are usually expensive in terms of their machine usage, and can in general be maintained by the software only for the numeric and coded parts of a DBMS+Text implementation, with a looser control of vocabulary in the text content.

How is data integrity maintained?

Does this apply to text as well as data?

The current SQL Standard includes an integrity enhancement feature, so most SQL conforming relational products are likely to include this facility - at least for the data domains - eventually.

Database integrity
Within any database of significant size a policing/audit role is required to inspect both the data and the control information to ensure its correctness. The structural integrity of the database can only be validated using specific utility software. Some vendors provide separate utility programs for this purpose.

What software is available to validate

- *the structural integrity of the database (ie pointers and control information for non relational products)?*

- *the data integrity of the database (ie data values and the relationships existing between them)?*

To correct non-data errors, some vendors provide diagnostic and fixing utilities. (The use of such facilities should be restricted to database administration staff only.)

In the event of an error being detected are facilities available to correct the error?

Sharing data

When multiple applications are operating concurrently, their update transactions must not interfere with each other. Two approaches are possible:

- predefine what resources are required, and suspend the application's initiation until they are available;

- allow applications to run concurrently and handle any contention if (and when) it arises.

Predefining the resources required is the most resource efficient method of handling shared concurrent access to data. Protected modes allow other run units to access the data but not to update it.

Which of the following modes of use can be allowed to a user (including a batch process) when modifying a database:

- *exclusive update (where no other users may attempt update at the same time)?*

- *protected update (where locking routines are provided to allow simultaneous updating but prevent conflicts)?*

- *non-protected update?*

- *protected retrieval (where the user is prevented from accessing a record subject to change)?*

- *non-protected retrieval (where the user is merely warned of a pending change - the normal TIMS provision)?*

To maximise information sharing, the unit of exclusion or locking ('granularity') should be small. However, this imposes significant performance and resource overheads, so usually some form of compromise is used - typically locking at the level of the TIMS unit of structure (record or section).

At what level of granularity can the TIMS lock units of the database to avoid update contention:

- *entire database?*
- *file?*
- *record?*
- *section?*
- *other?*

Space usage

The large volumes of disc space needed by TIMS applications may at least be controlled if the software has been well designed, and if appropriate tuning features are implemented. These include text and index compression; scavenging of unused space; and the use of 'stop words' to reduce the working search vocabulary.

Some approximate but useful design guides are:

- The average number of characters per word after removal of stopwords normally lies between 6 and 7 for English. This tends to increase somewhat in latin languages, and more sharply (maybe to 10 per word or more) in highly inflected or agglutinative languages (German, Finnish, Russian, Turkish);

- Character languages such as Chinese, Japanese and Korean appear to take up no more space than equivalent English translations, even when the 4-bytes per character CCCII representation is used;

- A short but carefully selected set of stop words can reduce the volume of text to be indexed by as much as 40% for English. In other European languages the effect may be less, if indefinite articles coincide with singular numerals (un, une;

um, uma etc) and text equivalents of small numbers are needed for searching;

- The annual production of a competent typist dedicated to text data entry is around ten million characters of new text, after allowing time for proof-reading and correction. A secretary supporting a group of three or four professionals normally generates three to five million characters per year, and a secretary to a single manager about two million.

See also section 1.5 of this volume under Text storage.

Text compression

In standard TIMS database designs, both the main text file and the inverse word list or concordance may be compressed, with space savings of up to 30%, or even more in special cases. (There are often incidental gains in retrieval performance also, as fewer disc accesses are made in searching.) A number of compression methods may be applied, but in all cases there is a trade-off between space saved and the added computer processing involved during both updates and retrievals.

Does the TIMS product offer compression of:

- *text files?*

- *index files?*

What is the effect of the increased processor load due to compression and decompression, on the maximum number of concurrent database users?

Is the compression method also applied to encryption of the text in the database (Chapter 8)?

Signature systems, with lower intrinsic overheads, offer very much less opportunity for space savings, and few instances of the application of compression techniques - even to the text file - have been recorded.

Scavenging

Most text databases undergo at least a few modifications and deletions, and some may replace substantial parts of the text over a period of a year. Two aspects of space control are important:

- As the database grows and the indexes mature, the space set aside for new words and for pointers to new occurrences will be taken up unevenly. Much of this spare space may be recoverable;

- Deleted text records leave spare space on disc. If the records really are deleted (and not merely marked as 'dead') then the space released may be recovered, both in the text file and in the indexes.

Is there provision for examination and adjustment of the growth space in the index files to allow adaption to the actual spare requirements as the database grows? Can the space be recovered?

Are 'deleted' records really removed from the text file and the space released, or merely marked as 'dead' or 'deleted'?

Can space released by deletions be recovered and reused:

- *automatically?*

- *by utility programs run by the DBA?*

Stop words

The selection of stop words is not straightforward, and it is often worth while to allow a database to grow to a moderate size before deciding which words should be selected. As few as ten stop words may be needed to effect large reductions in the indexes, but each should be examined with care before commitment. The following cases are only a small selection of those which can arise in particular applications: us = US; it = IT; or = OR; as = As; be = Be; in = In; p = P. Acronyms are a rich source of coincidences.

Is the stop word list 'standard' or may it be set up by the database administrator for each application?

Is there a facility to examine high frequency terms in the database as a tool for selection of stop words?

If a stop word is selected in error, can it be retrospectively reinserted without total re-indexing of the database?

Chapter 5
Performance

5.2 Interactive response

The technical aspects of design for good interactive response in TIMS applications are complex, and vendors have adopted a variety of practical solutions. In appraisal of products for performance-critical applications where diverse TIMS solutions are offered, reference may be made to one of the standard texts listed in Annex B.1 to ensure that vendors presentations are correctly interpreted. Further references to specific issues may be sought in the journals listed in Annex B.2 and the individual topic papers in Annex B.3. **Benchmark testing on realistic data sets with 'real life' queries is highly desirable for short-listed TIMS products in performance-critical applications.**

Storage related

The use of compression on database files, and of stop words to limit the need for indexing have some effect in improving response times as well as on storage (section 5.2). The frequency distribution of words found in a mature database often follows the curve shown in figure 5.1. (Adapted, with permission, from Ashford and Willett, 1989.)

In principle, it is possible to designate both very high frequency and very low frequency terms as stop words, since both groups have poor retrieval value for general inquiries. In practice, however, some high frequency terms are unavoidable - lawyers need 'act(s)' and engineers need 'steel(s)' in their search vocabularies. At the low frequency end, there may be terms which are productive for 'known item' retrieval, such as ISBN, ISSN, car registration number, NHS reference, in appropriate applications.

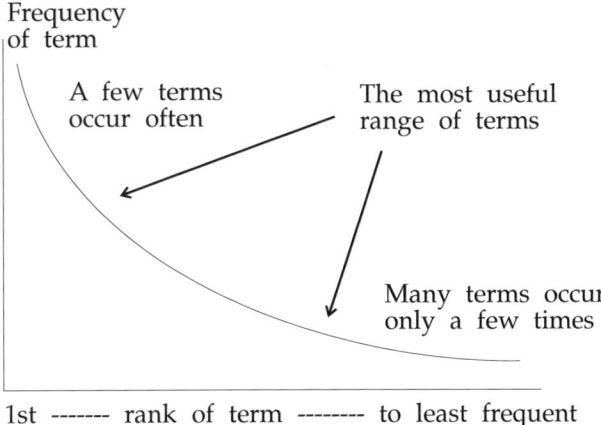

Figure 5.1: Typical curve for term frequency vs. rank

There is therefore a need for the query processor to deal with at least a significant minority of cases where one or more terms will be of high frequency in the database. The 'one off' terms in the database mainly affect the storage strategy.

What provision is made (apart from 'stop words') for dealing with a minority of high frequency terms in the database?

Indexing strategy

If facilities are provided for both vocabulary control and selective indexing of sections of the records, then for some applications these may be combined to improve retrieval performance. A designated section (for instance 'keywords') is used to hold controlled vocabulary words and bound phrases (chapter 2). These replace, for search purposes, phrase retrieval on high frequency terms in the raw text. Text sections may then, optionally, be left un-indexed, or, with some caution, the high frequency terms may be stopped.

Applications which fit this approach are found in pharmaceutical and biomedical sciences, transcriptions of public enquiries, and nuclear physics; among others.

Does the TIMS product provide both vocabulary control and selective indexing of sections of the text record?

The second aspect of indexing strategy which may have a major effect in databases with long text records is the choice between indexing at record level, or at word level. If searching on phrases is required, or the use of 'proximity' relations between words, then unless word level indexing is provided, a sequential search of the full text of the records is needed. This sequential search is central processor intensive, and may be a significant addition to the load of a multi-user system. It is always implied for signature systems, as only in this way can the software remove the small proportion of unintended retrievals ('false drops') which those systems generate.

Is word level indexing provided?

Query optimisation

Indexing - at least so far as it is normally provided in computer systems - exchanges actual work performed in preparing an alternative representation of part of a data set, for putative work which would otherwise have been performed in making sequential or heuristic searches. Because indexing is expensive in resources it is normally confined to those components of a data set for which a confident prediction of frequent use as access points can be made. Optimisation is concerned with making sure that for any particular query, best use is made of the previous investment in index production.

For DBMS, and for R.DBMS in particular, this subject is well known and there is a large literature. Date, 1986, argues that for R.DBMS at least, the high level language expression of searches makes a better performance achievable by the software - with full knowledge of operational statistics - than a human programmer could expect to achieve. For the non-text related parts of DBMS+Text software, the standard DBMS criteria apply - see Appraisal & Evaluation of Database Management Systems in this series.

For the text parts of DBMS+Text, and for standard inverse file TIMS, optimisation is less well defined. If the TIMS in question uses a 'sets' approach to query formulation (chapter 2 - indexed searching) then the whole task of optimisation is handed over to the on-line user, and effective performance depends on training, experience and individual perception. Typical 'rules' given to searchers include 'combine the low frequency terms first, and then any NOT terms, and then take in the high frequency terms'. (What the 'rule' omits is '. . . . and if you get nil returned, start over again differently'.)

In those TIMS where the whole query is normally expressed in a single command statement (directly, or via a user interface aid), the software has complete knowledge of the requirement and some degree of optimisation is usually possible. Even in sets-based systems, performance is sensitive to the way in which intermediate results are stored (or 'parked'), and this may become apparent during the 'combine' processing.

Does the TIMS provide for query optimisation on the text retrieval aspects of the database?

For DBMS+Text systems, is the query optimiser for normal searches extended to deal also with some or all parts of the text searches?

5.3 Batch performance

The addition of new text and the modification of existing records account for the major part of resource usage in TIMS applications. A few packages allow immediate, on-line updating of new records entered at the terminal, at a relatively high cost in central processor and disc channel usage for each insertion.

Update strategy

More commonly, a batch update process is used following one of two strategies.

- Some systems form a separate database for each tranche of new material, and then permit searching across all databases in the same ⌊family ꜰ. When the consequent run-time costs become noticeable, the databases are merged in a separate process into a single new set of files, and the cycle restarts.

- The alternative is to update a single database incrementally.

The effect is shown diagrammatically in Figure 5.2. (Adapted, with permission, from Ashford and Willett, 1989.)

Experience indicates that with few but large additions of new text, the 'separate files and merge' strategy usually comes out best. With small and frequent additions, the incremental approach gives lowest total costs.

What update approach has been adopted by the vendor?

Some TIMS have a range of options to improve the speed of batch updating, especially making use of the entire computer system when otherwise unused; allocating temporary extra buffer space; subdividing the update into several stages, each of which is optimised individually.

Does the TIMS offer high performance update in batch mode?

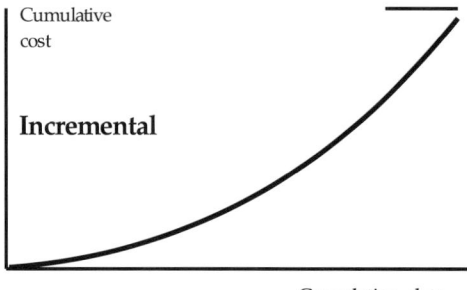

In the incremental update, each additional record costs just a little more than the last as the size of the inverse file and the list of pointers increase continuously. the horizontal cost bar (top right) is in the same position on each graph.

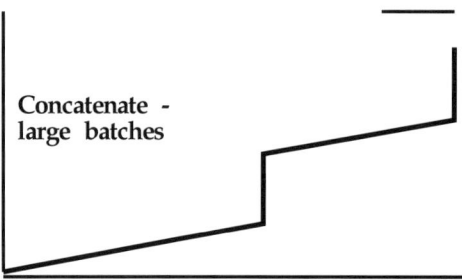

In *create new and concatenate*, each new add cycle adds a fixed increment of cost, puctuated by the occasional non-productive cost of a concenate run in batch mode. this case, with large, occasional lots of new records, is less costly over a period than incremental updating

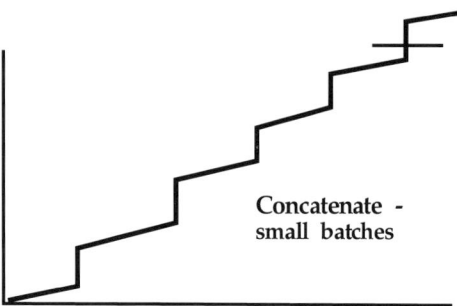

.... but when many small addition must be made, the opposite is true.

Figure 5.2: Alternative update strategy cost profiles

Chapter 5
Performance

Batch retrieval

For the production of large reports and bulletins, it is convenient to have the option to perform the retrievals in batch mode at times when equipment is lightly loaded. Some vendors provide specially adapted versions of the retrieval mode software for this purpose.

Can the TIMS retrieval software be run in batch mode?

Does the batch version offer better performance for large scale retrievals?

5.4 Application design

TIMS products are diverse compared with, for example, the relational DBMS packages, and are sometimes very sensitive to the way in which operational requirements are specified in the design phases of a project. In consequence, it is easy to introduce some unintentional effect in a non-critical part of the design specification, which may then bias the appraisal of one or another product.

It may, therefore, especially in large scale applications, be sensible to invite a short list of vendors to review the functional requirement as it affects their product, and allow them to suggest variations which will improve application performance. Any relaxation in the operational requirement must then, reasonably, be agreed with the user and offered to the other tenderers.

There are often gains from this approach in finding that some product can be made to fit especially well with the requirement. The off-setting complication is that any benchmark evaluations are then likely to be possible only at a high level, and detailed comparison of features will not be helpful.

Is the TIMS under appraisal sensitive to the detailed form of the requirement, and if so is consultation with the vendor on adjustments to the operational requirement appropriate?

Can bench mark tests be used to limit the extent to which all vendor proposals are constrained by the detail of the requirement?

Appraisal and Evaluation Library
Text-based Information Management Systems Volume

6 Special applications

Text-based information management systems have been around in some form for at least twenty years, and in that time several distinct sub-species have evolved adapted to particular application areas. The technology overlaps, sometimes considerably, with that of the general purpose TIMS which are the main concern of this volume, and in any particular case it may not be easy to determine whether the use of a standard TIMS product or of a more specialised application specific package will give better results.

This chapter therefore summarises the characteristics of several important special applications, and identifies the features which differentiate dedicated software products from TIMS in general. Two general points should be noted:

- If an organisation or department has a number of TIMS related applications, then there may be advantages in using a single, general purpose package to limit software diversity and related training and documentation costs, and put up with less than ideal performance on some special applications;

- The main limitation of the TIMS for special applications is usually that they are restricted in scope for manipulative data processing, such as recording of stock movements and other ephemeral data. This is less of a limitation in DBMS+Text products than in traditional narrative text TIMS.

Micro-computer versions of TIMS are included as special applications, because although they have been successfully installed for single user databases - small versions of mainframe or mini-computer packages - they are important also as the platform for a number of innovative developments. These include document production, optical disc archiving, and prototyping where the low cost and ease of start-up have proved major advantages.

6.1 Office environments

Office automation is a prolific source of texts in electronic form and appears to be a prime target for TIMS applications. In practice, there are many practical problems to be dealt with, and the development of successful applications requires careful planning. A typical office or administrative branch embodies a mix of inter-personal communications, dealings with 'outside world' contacts in a variety of forms, many in arbitrary formats, internal priorities and ad hoc schemes for dealing with local requirements, and, in the public service in particular, needs to adhere to registry and public record guidelines which must cover all, and not merely the more tractable electronic records.

The following points should be taken into account by the systems analyst, and the way in which they interact with TIMS or special purpose text management products reviewed:

- Some proportion of office paper, especially external, will be in hard copy format. The portion which includes brochures and visual display presentations is very difficult to convert to electronic media, and even typescript is not too easy (see Chapter 3). When a file is requested for study, however, both electronic and paper records are normally of interest, and the dual presentation is not easy.

- Much office and administrative paper is ephemeral, and practical experience suggests that more than 50% of pages generated in OA systems can be discarded within six months (drafts; meetings notices; travel arrangements; cumulative progress reports; press releases from other bodies and similar materials). This leads to a requirement for effective 'weeding' systems which will distinguish between discards and material which should be relegated to registry storage or sent to archive.

- Secretaries and typists carry files of re-usable or revisable papers (monthly reports; answers to repetitious Parliamentary Questions) in local storage on word processors. These, and other

Chapter 6
Special applications

'personal' collections can be quite extensive, but are accessed by user knowledge, and are rarely formally indexed. When staff change, they tend to become unusable and may be discarded.

- The 'file and folder' classification systems characteristic of word processing systems appear to work in practice for up to about ten groups of ten folders each. This may represent 5 - 10 Mb of original text, or one to two years' work for a busy secretary. Above this scale, the systems become cumbersome, and the lack of subject information beyond the general file titles can lead to prolonged searches - more awkward in electronic form than by paging through filed sheets.

  If TIMS systems are to assist with this aspect of local filing, they must be able to accept both group/folder headings and the 'profiles' of documents provided by the word processing software. If the discipline of setting up document profiles with suitable subject keywords has not been put in place, then there are hidden costs of re-indexing at the time of transfer to a database.

Many of the systems so far implemented which are regarded as successful by their users have been restricted to a single, large volume class of office paper, and often to material where the whole database can readily be got into a standard electronic format. Standard TIMS software, often with highly non-standard translation utilities for markup removal, has been successfully applied, in one or other of the English speaking countries, to committee records; journals of legislative assemblies; press releases; texts of PQs; inquiry transcripts; texts of frequently changed regulations and guidelines; health and safety papers; personnel records. The 'general filing' has proved, on the whole, intractable, except as a limited facet of records management (section 6.3).

Some computer system vendors have produced 'office system' products as part of their standard software range - for example, All-in-1 on DEC VMS computers, CEO on DG AOS, ISPF on IBM MVS, and PROFS on IBM VM/CMS. TIMS vendors, in response, have produced interfaces to these products so that they may run within the office system environment, and act as indexed repositories for selected documents. Subject to the difficulties noted above, these integrated interfaces may be of considerable help in making a TIMS application readily acceptable to office users.

Does the vendor offer 'office system' integration?

Is this a standard feature, or a chargeable extra?

6.2 Libraries and information centres

Many special libraries have installed catalogue systems based on TIMS software, and government departments have been among the leaders. Other applications have included bibliographic databases of the literature relevant to the work of the department, patents, standards, research reports and similar materials. These are typically medium to large scale reference databases, of indicative text records.

Special applications rise where the library or information centre wishes to add to the reference system a range of library 'housekeeping' procedures. These would typically include ordering, acquisitions and accession of new titles, recording of serials as they are delivered (and prompting of defaulters), loans of library stock and recovery of overdue items, and reservations of books and journals for readers. At small transaction volumes, these can often be incorporated as extensions to the TIMS applications, and a number of commercial products have 'library management' extensions.

On a larger scale, however, it may be preferable to use a library management directed software product, and accept reduced flexibility in information retrieval. The choice turns on the processing limitations of TIMS products, and the complexity of detailed requirements which may arise in a larger library. A particular complication may arise if the library is committed to the use of ISO 2709/MARC record formats for bibliographic data (see section 1.2 - special formats) which tend to be intractable in general purpose text retrieval systems. Kimberley, 1990, lists many library automation products, suitable at all scales from microcomputers to mainframes.

Chapter 6
Special applications

Does the operational requirement indicate that library automation specialised products should also be considered?

6.3 Records management

This is an area of current development, especially as the importance of BS 5750 - Quality Systems (ISO 9000) is being increasingly recognised. In records management the problems of documents in diverse formats from many sources which were noted for office automation are now manifest, and indicative text (ITX) solutions have so far been most used.

For large scale registries, and especially for archives where the identification of individual documents of high value is important, standard TIMS products have been successfully applied. If traffic in files is heavy, then the same housekeeping problems of loan recording and file recovery noted for libraries may recur, and either the extension of the TIMS software, a hybrid solution, or a move to special purpose records management products may be indicated. There is always a significant investment in user interfaces, both to serve occasional searchers who are not practised with the system, and also to guide even regular users through the complex of document formats and classification practices which normally builds up over a few years.

For small scale applications, a dedicated records management package running on a micro-computer may be a sound alternative, as the text retrieval needs are less demanding, and for small organisations, a last resort sequential search through a number of 'possible' files for a lost document is not too daunting. Kimberley, 1990, contains a number of products.

Does the operational requirement indicate that records management specialised products should also be considered?

6.4 Electronic publishing

The publication of texts and compound documents in electronic form may involve the selection of items from large databases of reference material. So far, this has been applied mainly to bibliographic sources such as Chemical Abstracts and Excerpta Medica, and the search keys have usually been controlled vocabulary classification codes. In some cases standard TIMS

103

software products are applied, in others special purpose systems using much the same principles.

The rapid spread of CD-ROM as a medium, and the advent of CDI, appear likely to lead to growth and diversity in new applications. TIMS will be applicable for those cases:

- where bibliographic references on a subject sub-set are derived from a larger, general database;

- where portions of full text can be selected and assembled from a large reference set into a special publication. Maintenance and software manuals are being considered for this approach;

- where numbers of scientific and technical reports are available in electronic form, and material can be selected and presented in support of patent applications, regulatory submissions, or educational or 'briefing' documents.

Use of TIMS is unlikely to be effective when the publication is composed as a 'one off' intellectual product, unless the document itself comes to be a searchable database in its own right - SEDBASE on side effects of drugs, or Hansard Oral Questions (HOQ), of the Canada House of Commons.

6.5   Micro-computers

The developing central processor power of micro-computers and the availability of large, cheap storage units have made the use of these machines for text-based information systems increasingly realistic over the last three years. Most TIMS products available on micros, and most micro-based work-stations for use with mainframe TIMS have so far used the IBM PC or its analogues, but the Macintosh range is becoming more important, especially in compound document applications and may be expected to be seen more in new software.

The following discussion is based mainly on IBM PC and MS-DOS operating system environments, but much of it can also be applied directly to Macintosh equipment, or to small RISC machines (Reduced

Chapter 6
Special applications

Instruction Set Computers) running UNIX or one of its dialects. Larger UNIX systems with substantial multi-user capability do not fit here and should be considered with the mainframe and mini-computer TIMS dealt with in the other chapters.

Small and single user applications

Some of the major TIMS products have excellent micro-computer versions, which embody the majority of the functionality of the mainframe or mini-computer software from which they were derived. There are also many packages available only on micro-computers, of uneven quality, and with variable chances of commercial survival (see listings in Kimberley, 1990). Examination of products advertised suggests that of those TIMS available on micro-computers only, about 10% disappear and are replaced by new names annually.

Technical limitations arise mainly in the file sizes which can be directly addressed by MS-DOS, and which the TIMS file management system may have to circumvent, and in the capacity of the relatively slow processors and disc input/output channels to deal with large text additions in a reasonable time.

Can the planned application volumes be handled by the file system:

- *for disc space?*

- *for update times when text is added?*

The features which are likely to be lost in transfer of TIMS software from mini-computer to micro include real-time updating of records; multi-user access, especially for writing to the database; thorough security controls (MS-DOS weaknesses); and flexibility in screen layout design. The last point may be reversed in the case of moves from mainframes where a gain in presentation quality is often realised.

Sub-set systems

In some applications, it is useful to maintain a large database centrally, but transfer sub-sets to branches where the selected part will be heavily used. This has several benefits, namely, saving on communications traffic to remote sites; easing problems with security over telecommunications networks; and allowing local autonomy in developing ancillary presentation and publication services. Occasional enquiries needing the whole database are then dealt with either by remote access, or by (secure) electronic mail enquiry to a member of support staff at the centre.

Can sub-sets of the database be transferred from a central mainframe or mini-computer system?

Is it necessary to re-index the transferred files, or can the indexes be sub-set and transferred also?

If optical disc storage of related images is involved, then the advantages of holding copy stores locally and avoiding heavy communications traffic may be considerable. A few micro-computer versions of TIMS products have specially developed 12 cm optical disc interfaces, both to CD-ROM and to WORMs.

Local area networks

An alternative to sharing use of a TIMS on a mini-computer or mainframe, is to install the text database at a node of a local area network (LAN) and give access to other LAN users. In a LAN environment, the most difficult technical problem is that of controlling conflicting modifications to the database from different points. Security control depends at least as much on the LAN version in use as on the TIMS software.

The main system structures in current implementations are:

- Copies of both database and software are 'broadcast' to all LAN users who need them. Updating is done on the source system only, and all other users have 'read only' versions. This is a simple approach for small databases, but is wasteful in storage and may incur multiple copy charges for software;

- The database and TIMS software are held on a single node, and one LAN user at a time may have access. For lightly used applications, where access conflicts are easily resolved, this is easy to implement. A few products allow the single node

Chapter 6
Special applications

TIMS database to have one 'write' user and several 'read only' user, but these are generally confined to UNIX based networks;

- A LAN 'server' node may hold the database files and sometimes the file access and write conflict resolution procedures, which are then accessed using copies of the rest of the TIMS software on each user station. This appears to be the least costly and most versatile solution, but is not yet widely available.

Developments in 'client/server' structures are being actively discussed by several vendors, mainly for LAN environments, but also for star networks on some mini-computers.

What LAN configurations are offered?

Is the LAN security provision compatible with that provided with the TIMS product, and with application requirements?

How is the system to be recovered if LAN failures occur during read only access? and during updates?

Can a user on a LAN interrupt a search which has been launched on another node, and is proving to take an excessively long time? How is this accomplished?

Can auxiliary optical disc storage units be mounted on the same LAN to provide compound document access?

Secure applications

Small scale, secure TIMS systems may conveniently be set up on micro-computers, and kept within access-controlled premises. Such systems are also, subject to proper controls, portable, for applications which require this facility.

Are micro-computer based configurations available which are suitable for local secure systems?

Can these systems be transported to other sites without loss of control over security?

Prototyping

One of the most important applications for micro-computer version of TIMS software intended for mainframe or mini-computer use is in the setting up of development prototypes.

It is a common experience of systems analysts working in this field that end users find it difficult to express their requirements clearly without 'hands-on' experience of a system which is at least partially right. Since micro-computer versions are always cheaper, often quicker to implement and revise - especially when updating and security aspects can be deferred - they have been effectively used as a development and specification tool. Useful features are:

- template designs; command files ready to modify; pre-installed directories with temporary file names; automatic space allocation;

- direct compatibility of record and command language formats between micro-computer and larger system versions;

- 'forms' or similar aids to quick interface design;

- vendor supplied 'test' or 'demonstration' databases of a reasonable number of records of different types;

- session logging facilities to record the actual paths taken and the frequencies as users learn to handle the prototype versions.

Shared experience through a user group may be especially valuable at the prototyping stage, especially if the systems analysts involved have only limited experience of working with TIMS applications.

What facilities are provided to aid prototyping?

7 Recent technical developments

This chapter serves two purposes. It introduces, very briefly, a number of developing topics which are likely to become important in TIMS systems during the next few years. These range from 'just emerging from research as credible for use in practice' to 'proven but not yet widely implemented'. The majority of TIMS users in the last ten years have tended to be technically conservative, for example in the adherence of librarians to the MARC (ISO 2709) format standard. A general slow response to innovation appears to be changing as computer scientists and system developers take up wider challenges, and it is difficult to predict which new ideas will first find practical uses on a large scale.

The second purpose is to collect together a number of hardware related TIMS developments for which the general selection criteria are not too helpful, so that these are not overlooked when the circumstances in which they are cost-effective solutions arise. Some of these, such as the ICL CAFS processors, are well established; others, like transputer farms, are just beginning to find working applications in text retrieval.

These are pointers to the future, and indications for systems analysts. No attempt has been made to be exhaustive, and no formal criteria or standard questions are practicable at this stage of most developments. The references in Annex B provide further information, Salton (1989) and Willett (1988) for general accounts, and the journal articles for more specific topics.

7.1 Hypertext

Hypertext represents information in a diversity of formats as a set of 'cards' on which topics are placed. The contents are normally accessed by navigating along links between pairs of cards. The links are established by editorial choice in some sense, but may represent hierarchical or (commonly) network relationships among the data cards.

The 'content' of the cards may be text, tables, graphic drawings, raster images, or ports through which sound or video sequences are played. In a few products it is also possible to use a card as an access window to operating systems, telecommunications interfaces, or to application programs. Hypertext has been applied as an integrating 'harness' for mixed computer and media systems, but generally on a small scale. A few products offer text retrieval on the content of cards using normal inverse file indexes.

Problems with hypertext systems stem from the costs of development and editorial control, and from the need to provide 'maps' of the data content so that users do not become lost within the system. A more subtle danger is that the editor's choice of access points and linkages can bias the presentation in a way which would be evident in text but is concealed in a hypertext presentation where the user sees only a small segment at a time. Doland (1989) deals with this and related subjects.

It is not clear whether the widespread enthusiasm of computer scientists and academic psychologists will be reflected in a corresponding scale of working applications.

7.2 'Intelligent' interfaces

During the last three years there has been both a rapid increase in commercial awareness of information retrieval research, and a less marked series of innovative software products. Most of the practical products are concerned with assisting users of databases to improve the effectiveness of their searches, by making the presentation more sympathetic, by improving retrieval performance, or by automating some aspects of skilled judgement.

In the following sections, examples of available commercial products are described briefly to illustrate what may be expected. These are only some of the available packages.

Ranking & relevance

The idea of ranking of results is to present the user with the results of searches in a sequence where the most relevant come first. This means that over-retrieval is no longer such a problem, and search

Chapter 7
Recent technical developments

criteria can be made wider to reduce the possibility of missing significant documents.

Criteria are necessary for ranking, and may take the form of weights attached to search terms, or of values derived from user judgements as to the relevance of members of an initial set of retrieved documents.

STATUS/IQ (incorporated in new releases of STATUS) is one of only a few commercial products. It is based on research into retrieval from full text legal databases in Australia, but is proving much more widely applicable. It uses the classic Sparck-Jones / Robertson measure of document relevance as a key parameter in evaluating the results of searches, and overcomes the a priori difficulty of estimating relevance ratios for any particular search by proceeding from a heuristic allocation of provisional weights to search terms, and an iterative re-evaluation of the intermediate weights. Paragraphs, rather than whole documents are treated as the working units for information content, and in a structured document selected sections (title, abstract etc) can also be selectively weighted. The context of a search term is used as well as its relative frequency in determining its value. The knowledge requirement about the subject domain is kept to a minimum, and expressed in rules about association of words and phrases, and expansion rules for generic terms.

During a search a user enters natural language queries, which STATUS/IQ parses and reforms as sets of boolean strings. At any point the user can ask to see what is going on 'under the covers' for reassurance. The queries are used to retrieve a set of relevant documents - sometimes quite large - which is then ranked in descending order of relevance. The user may then view the top few records, browse freely, or inspect and vary the weights allocated to search components or to structural sections of the documents. Searches may be stored for repeated use (CA/SDI applications) or applied to document stream analysis. (Pape and Jones, 1988.)

Menu processors

A number of approaches to making user interfaces more responsive and helpful are being implemented, so far on a small scale. CANSEARCH and its successor MENUSE (see Ashford and Willett, 1989) offer vocabulary aid in searching biomedical TIMS. OKAPI (Walker, 1988) sets out to improve subject retrieval effectiveness in dealing with on-line catalogues. One commercial example is described below.

TOME (TOME Associates Limited) is a search aid based on research in the University of London. It uses well established artificial intelligence techniques to develop, for a given subject domain, a knowledge base of the domain content. Users' questions are analysed and reformatted, ambiguities are removed through dialogue, and the queries are finally formulated as boolean or other query forms on one or more databases chosen to match the query. Results may be sorted by a number of simple criteria.

TOME is very powerful in guiding users of diverse experience through complex retrievals in specialist knowledge domains. It requires, however, a considerable investment in 'knowledge engineering' to set up the domain rules and the supporting data tables for any particular application. It is unlikely, therefore, to be cost effective for wide ranging subject fields, except possibly as an aid to external database searching where the 'knowledge' content is of the workings of the database systems and of their scope lists, rather than the referred matter.

Concept retrieval

The products in this group are based on setting up a pre-determined set of 'concept' criteria for the 'relevance' of a document to a particular requirement ('topic'). The initial research system (as RUBRIC) was directed to the use of 'evidence assessment' algorithms to match pre-determined 'concept' structures to a stream of text messages. TOPIC is a current commercial implementation, using somewhat simpler algorithms. It assumes a stable search set, and a well defined user population. This is typical of news and intelligence gathering, and it is significant that the CIA and Reuters are cited as major users (Tong et al., 1989).

The 'concepts' are defined using a combination of hierarchic classes; subject terms; boolean format 'rules', and weights attached to particular facets. Terms from retrieved documents may be added to the concept definition. Searches may be made on input streams, marking 'wanted' documents with their appropriate category, or retrospectively, on cumulated full text databases. The results from searches are ranked, based on goodness of fit between the document and the weighted concept expression.

There will be, for any real application, a significant investment in a concept library. In a volatile application area, the task might become difficult to sustain. While concept based searching can be demonstrated to look straightforward, the good results which are attainable probably require a fair level of sophistication in information theory.

7.3 Signatures in VLDB

Signature storage and retrieval for very large databases has for some years been a research topic at the Royal Melbourne Institute of Technology and the University of Melbourne (Sacks-Davis, 1983, and Salton, 1989). Extension of 'large database' studies to 'data plus text' has resulted in a commercial product - TITAN - which runs successfully on UNIX systems.

It uses a two-level application of signatures, to individual records and to blocks of records. These are superimposed during retrieval to achieve fast and accurate results, and the small number of 'false drops' are removed as the records are called up for inspection.

Positive reasons for consideration include:

- Large databases (over 1 gigabyte) of short to medium (up to 2,000 bytes) records with a mixture of text and data;

- Stable databases of structured records, with controlled language at a field level;

- Typical retrieved sets in the region of 20 to 100 records.

For such applications as large taxonomic databases, this technology has delivered very fast retrievals on large collections. The main limitations are:

- Few 'language related' aids, such as truncation, are practicable, although stemming may be applied;

- Amendment and deletion of records is expensive.

Similar products are emerging in North America, but at the time of writing (early 1991) TITAN appears to be the only member of this class marketed and supported in Europe.

7.4 Hardware searching

The high text acquisition and indexing costs of inverted file TIMS software, and the retrieval limitations of signature methods have long been recognised. They are, however, unlikely to be avoided completely in any conventional computer architecture intended for general purpose application. There have been, however, several alternative approaches using hardware-based alternatives.

Database machines

Database machines form a class of computer which has been developed specifically for the purposes of database scanning. Most of these machines provide content addressability by associating processing logic with the read/write heads of a disc unit to allow database searching and processing activities that would otherwise have been performed by the central processor of the host machine. Several small search processors are usually provided, each executing the same search and processing commands on different parts of the database, and this parallelism further reduces the time required.

Probably the most widely installed machine of this type is the ICL Content Addressable Filestore. CAFS is standard across the entire ICL mainframe range for both data and text scanning. It consists of a cooperating group of special hardware units operating in conjunction with a conventional disk controller. While the latter continues to be responsible for normal

Chapter 7
Recent technical developments

file transfers in which data is either read or written in blocks, the CAFS units scan stored data in a continuous stream from disk, and pass back to the host only that small sub-set of the data stream that satisfies the query specified by the user.

CAFS is normally embedded in application-oriented software products, and includes relational DBMS links. For TIMS there are two main implementations. In ICLFILE, documents in revisable format (ODA) are held on magnetic disc in a 'file and folder' structure, and profiles, or short catalogue entries, of each document are placed in a CAFS file. The office user then has a simple form-filling way of quickly searching the profiles of a large document set through CAFS, while the original text body is kept in an appropriate form for re-use. Documents for long term retention may be transferred to STATUS as they move from office use to archive.

INDEPOL, which bridges the gap between data and text, was originally developed as a CAFS based storage and retrieval system for police and defence information systems - and in consequence has particularly strong and flexible provisions for access security and for direct use by professional staff. It has also been widely applied to credit assessment and fraud investigations, and to air safety inquiries. CAFS is used to treat data fields and text alike as access points for searching, and uses a simple, relational-like dialogue or a form filling enquiry mode to make search formulation easier.

Consider database machines such as CAFS for:

- An alternative to software TIMS in existing ICL series 29xx and 39xx installations which are considering taking on TIMS applications;

- Frequently updated, fast response, mixed data and text applications of 100 Mb per database or less;

- High security TIMS systems.

Array processors

Parallelism in the CAFS system is implemented in the key channels and multiplexed data stream. A more extreme example of the use of parallel processing techniques for text retrieval is demonstrated by recent work on the class of parallel computers known as array processors which contain a large, two-dimensional array of identical and very simple processing elements, or PEs. The basic design of an array processor allows all of the PEs to carry out the same operation in parallel. Each PE is linked to four neighbours and can read data from their stores. Row and column highways are provided to connect together sets of PEs in the array.

The control unit of an array processor carries out many of the functions of the control unit of a conventional computer in that it is responsible for the tasks of instruction fetch, decode and modify by registers. Most of the decoded instructions are sent to the array of PEs; each PE then executes the instruction sequence on its own locally held data.

An array processor developed and supported in UK which has been applied to text retrieval is the AMT (formerly ICL) Distributed Array Processor, or DAP (Reddaway, 1988).

Transputer networks

An alternative type of parallelism is exemplified by Multiple Instruction stream, Multiple Data stream, or MIMD, computers. Here, the parallelism arises from the fact that some, or many, processors can execute their own program simultaneously, while being able to communicate between themselves to meet the requirements of a particular application. An example of a series of microprocessors which has been developed in UK specifically for parallel processing, and applied to text searching, is the INMOS Transputer.

The availability of transputer networks seems to make serial text scanning a realistic prospect even on microcomputer systems, where the network could be used as a hardware accelerator to improve the performance of the basic host machine. The network is organised as a processor farm, or processor pool. Each transputer runs the same program as the other members of the network, but on a different subset of the input data stream. The basic computational task

Chapter 7
Recent technical developments

which needs to be carried out by each processor is the matching of a set of query keyword stems against a document title and abstract. A query-document pair is distributed to the transputers in the pool as soon as there is a transputer available to process it.

This is a highly efficient way of using a network for applications involving relatively little inter-processor communication relative to the computational load. Such systems are likely to become increasingly cost effective with the rapidly falling costs of parallel hardware of all sorts.

7.5 High density media

The large volumes of storage associated with TIMS systems make high density media an interesting option for storage of stable files.

For large file storage, that is, using standard operating system input / output protocols, consider:

- WORM discs at 12 cm or 30 cm sizes for database storage of 120 Mb and 2.4 Gb respectively;

- Rewritable optical discs if they become substantially cheaper per byte than magnetic discs;

- WORM discs or digital optical paper for backup and archives.

For hybrid systems including images, the TIMS software is likely to be associated with one particular make of WORM disc and its supporting interfaces and software.

Appraisal and Evaluation Library
Text-based Information Management Systems Volume

8 Control and Security

For all non-trivial systems it is important to control the development and operation of the system, and the structure and content of the database. Such control depends to a large extent on the facilities provided by the TIMS or any associated DBMS. For special considerations affecting DBMS applications, see *Appraisal & Evaluation of Database Management Systems* in this series.

Text databases introduce a special security problem both in themselves and particularly when the results of searches are transmitted to remote sites, in that natural language material is generally comprehensible in its stored form, and so is directly exposed to unauthorised access. This is more serious than for DBMS material which, except for formatted reports, is usually uninterpretable without a schema or data dictionary to assemble data elements in a meaningful way.

8.1 Ownership

Databases must have been created; the person who did this is the 'owner' (DBO) and may consequently have special rights over the database. Databases also need to be administered and in general this requires a Database Administrator (DBA).

Control over who can do what with a database, both for the end users and system developers, will be vested in an individual, usually the DBO or the DBA.

Who controls the database? Can this individual delegate his authority or elements of it?

8.2 Control over access

Shared text databases are likely to contain data which is not updatable by certain classes of users. If a database is to contain confidential data then access to such data may also be forbidden. Commonly provided access control facilities include the ability to define user groups (to allocate common privileges to them), the ability to control specific classes of command (such as update commands) and the ability to hide sub-files or chapters, whole documents, or sections of documents from view.

Access controls may be initially restricted (that is, the default being not to allow access and the access control being set to permit access) or they may be restrictive by subsequent settings. The latter form of control is more common. Note that DBMS-provided facilities to control access at occurrence (record or data item) level are rare; if provided, they are usually implemented using DBA-specified database procedures This level of control is commoner, almost standard, in traditional TIMS products.

What access control facilities are provided for

- *the entire database?*

- *major logical sections of the database (for example records, sections or files)?*

- *(for DBMS components) data views, sub-schemas or tables (record types)?*

- *other divisions?*

Can the restrictions or privileges be assigned to groups of users, or only to individual users?

If text in documents is to be kept concealed from some users, then it is important that the word lists or vocabulary files should be similarly constrained. Otherwise a user with limited access can use a view of the vocabulary to establish that certain terms exist only in inaccessible sections, may be able to deduce some part of the contents, and may be led to attempt access to material which would have better remained unknown. It is also important for record and section level restrictions to operate consistently during indexed or browsing access, including renumbering of sub-files or chapters, and of records within sequences to avoid declaring the existence of invisible data.

Is vocabulary access consistent with controls on record or section access?

Are the restrictions on indexed and browsing access consistent?

Procedures can be made more sophisticated than simple passwords. There are particular complications

Chapter 8
Control and security

with UNIX based systems, as the control of logon and password procedures varies from one dialect of UNIX to another, and sites which run many applications on one machine, or on a closely connected network must develop consistent access protocols for all users to avoid inadvertent security breach at shell level.

Are access controls confined to simple passwords or can the DBA-specified procedures be invoked to validate user passwords?

Are UNIX environments adequately secure for the particular TIMS implementation?

In a controlled environment, attempted access control violations should at least be logged. In a secure environment, it may be necessary to inform the DBA and to disconnect the user's terminal.

What action is taken by the TIMS on an attempted access control violation?

The TIMS may be required to log all database accesses. Processing the audit trail can provide information regarding access patterns and attempted security violations.

What information can the DBMS log to provide an audit trail of database activity?

What facilities can be used to query logs of use, attempted security and other violations?

8.3 Security planning	CCTA advocate use of CRAMM - the CCTA Risk Analysis and Management Methodology, as an element of the planning for Information Systems. CRAMM reviews the requirements for security, including those associated with use of TIMS and DBMS, in a more complete manner than can be included in this document, and can be used to draw up appropriate criteria and questions, for inclusion in the evaluation model.

Appraisal and Evaluation Library
Text-based Information Management Systems Volume

9 Portability

Portability as a strategic objective for Text-based Information Management Systems can be considered at several levels. These include portability of the TIMS product, of the structures and parsing rules, of the data, and of the skills of the applications developers and users. If a TIMS-with-DBMS hybrid is being considered, or a DBMS+Text system, then portability considerations for DBMS should also be taken into account (see *Appraisal & Evaluation of Database Management Systems* in this series).

9.1 TIMS portability

It is necessary to establish what particular environments are supported. Separate lists of operating systems and compatible word processors may not be particularly helpful, as not every word processor will operate under every operating system.

On what machine/operating system combinations does the product run?

Do all of these alternative environments support compatible character sets and user work-stations?

Is this flexibility reduced when vector graphics or bit-mapped components must be included in compound documents?

Products often take advantage of specific features of an environment. These features which may not be available on another system include for TIMS, operating system gateways, word processor text filters, record locking procedures for multi-user updating.

Does the TIMS take advantage of specific features of the environment?

9.2 Data portability

Adoption of multiple text-based information management systems based on the same TIMS usually allows data to be ported between sites with different operational platforms with few problems. Unless the system software and database environments are identical, porting of data will involve a database unload/reload operation. Factors such as implementation specific character sets or collating sequences may cause problems.

What mechanisms are available for exporting/importing data?

Do the different environments on which the TIMS is supported have common character set, collating sequences, parse rules?

The use of the same database on different sites with different TIMS products is sometimes feasible. It depends on a number of factors, such as record structure compatibility, similarity of command language, and often the use of a small set of common retrieval facilities. The European Common Command Language (CCL) is, in principle, indistinguishable to the user across diverse systems on which it is implemented. This should be checked for each specific instance where it might be applied. Some TIMS can, through macro-processor facilities or command files, simulate the command vocabularies of others.

Does the TIMS offer command language variation or CCL to allow databases on different platforms and software to maintain partial compatibility?

Is the TIMS in question one of those for which there are very similar competitors, adapted to different platforms?

Does the vendor provide database transfer or translation utilities to other TIMS products?

It is unlikely that thesaurus facilities, macro-processors and performance tuning aids will be compatible across TIMS.

9.3 Skill mobility

Application skill mobility between sites (if required) will be maximised if a common system and application environment is chosen.

To what extent does the product support skill mobility?

9.4 Downloading

TIMS users often rely on 'downloading', that is the extraction of one or more records from a database, for

Chapter 9
Portability

transfer to other uses. The other use in question is typically a micro-computer based TIMS system in which records are enhanced or specialised for local purposes. This common sub-application requires record structure markers to be accessible and transferrable with the text data.

Are record structures suitable for downloading?

Are any other downloading aids provided in the TIMS?

Appraisal and Evaluation Library
Text-based Information Management Systems Volume

10 Product credibility

Text-based information management systems are, like DBMS, frequently the subject of 'imaginative' marketing and it is important to establish the extent to which sales claims are likely to be borne out in practice. For well-established products, the practical value of consulting existing users is high, although the reluctance of managements to admit to serious selection errors should be recognised in assessing visit reports.

Some TIMS are produced by small or relatively unknown software houses or are written and supported in foreign countries and marketed here by agents. Others are new to the market-place and are therefore as yet untried. Such products are not necessarily unsatisfactory, but it is important to assess the likelihood of the software and the vendor still being viable in the future before committing to using the product, irrespective of its technical merit.

10.1 Product quality

Text-based information management systems should ideally be constructed to a high quality using rigorous, structured development and testing techniques. This is, at present, not the case for many technically and commercially viable products, and the application of formal methods to the older TIMS will take place only slowly. Some level of quality assurance can however reasonably be sought:

Does the product developer subscribe to and comply with the requirements of British Standard (BS) 5750 or equivalent? (This deals with a supplier's capabilities to operate a quality management system in the design, manufacture, installation, inspection and testing of a product).

Has the product been submitted to any independent authority (for example the National Computing Centre Ltd (NCC)) for evaluation or certification/validation? If so, are the results available? Are any independently reached performance figures available from such authorities?

What guarantees are there against defects in the product?

10.2 Product development

Information on the development status of the product is essential before making a long term commitment to its use.

What is the current development stage of the product, for example:

- *static?*
- *stable but in the process of being cosmetically enhanced?*
- *being functionally enhanced?*
- *in the process of being developed for use on other machines?*

Have any enhancements been introduced recently? Are there any which are under development? What are these planned enhancements and the target dates for their introduction?

When was the last major, new version (as defined by the supplier) released and when is the next major, new version planned for release?

How does the company determine when a system requires enhancement and the nature of the additional or supplementary facilities and features which are to be incorporated?

Are there any weaknesses which have been identified in the current version of the product?

What plans are there for the product over next 3 to 5 years? Will the product be different to today's version? If so, what differences will there be?

Have any overseas products been Anglicized (for example date format, £ symbol)? Are general European character sets (including, for example é, É, ü, å, ø, ç) available?

How many updates have been issued in the last year? Were these innovative versions, or problem fixes?

10.3 Supplier assessment

The supplier assessment will take into account the size of the supplier, whether they are the originators of the software or simply agents, how long they have been producing or marketing software, the size and whether they are a company based in Britain or abroad.

Chapter 10
Product credibility

Some TIMS were produced originally by small independent software houses and then marketed, sometimes under another name, by system vendors. These may suffer from poor access to full technical support. Others have been developed for use within an information handling organisation, and later been packaged and marketed. In this case there are the advantages of close awareness of user needs, and possible disadvantages of inexperience in a competitive marketplace.

Standard information to support judgements in this area comprises:

Name, address and telephone number of supplier.

Name(s), position(s), address(es) and telephone number(s) of the person(s) to contact for further details, if necessary, regarding

- *Marketing information*
- *Technical support.*

How long has the company been in operation

- *in the UK?*
- *world-wide?*

Was the product originally developed by the above supplier?

What organisations have used the supplier's services in the past?

Does the supplier have a range of products covering related topics, that is, is it an area in which he specialises?

Is the supplier a subsidiary of any other company?

How many years has the supplier been active in the development and/or marketing of TIMS?

During the last year, what proportion of total revenue has been derived from TIMS?

How many employees are dedicated to the development of text-based information management systems? How many have information science qualifications?

What percentage of total profit or income has been contributed to research and development of TIMS? (that is future facilities, compound document architectures, optical disc storage, etc)

10.4 Product background Most information management systems start their life in a slightly unstable state; some never achieve stability. If a TIMS has a reasonable number of production field sites (not simply copies out for approval, or copies distributed but not seriously used), then the product's capabilities and potential may be assumed to be at least adequate and the uncertainty involved in selecting such a product is less than that of a new and untried package. New releases of an established product may however be troublesome.

Development ancestry Potential buyers should establish when the 'product' was first available rather than the concept. Some text-based information management systems are developments of tools used internally by the supplier. Sometimes these early internal versions are quoted to imply that the product has a longer 'history' than is the case.

When was the TIMS first installed at a customer site for customer use?

What is the source and history of product(s) under consideration?

For how long has the TIMS been commercially available?

What was the original development environment (that is the machine on which the TIMS was developed in the supplier's organisation)?

What is the present development environment?

Did the vendor write the software, or is he acting as agent?

Where is the software originator based, for example local, UK, Europe, America?

Development profile Many TIMS are still in a state of development and enhancement. New features, facilities and

Chapter 10
Product credibility

environments are being added. While this may provide many useful new features it may cause problems if releases with desirable new features appear during a development. If migration to a new release requires re-indexing of existing databases, then substantial computer time costs may be incurred.

Note that new versions of text-based information management systems usually incorporate significant improvements either in functionality or in performance. New versions are typically released on a 12 to 24 month cycle. Intermediate releases tend towards fixing 'bugs' only.

How frequently are major product versions released?

What enhancements, if any, are planned for the TIMS and when will they be introduced?

What is supplier policy towards compatibility between versions?

How does the TIMS supplier determine when a system requires enhancement and the nature of the additional/supplementary facilities which are to be incorporated?

Is there an established channel for coordination and feedback of product improvement requests from the User Group? Does the vendor take account of these requests in a reasonable time?

Product usage

The numbers of active users of a TIMS, the sales profile of the product and other sources such as product appraisal and evaluation reports can give valuable indications of scope, applicability and commercial viability.

How many user sites of the TIMS are there, of comparable application scale and functional content:

- *in the UK?*
- *within Government?*
- *outside Government?*
- *elsewhere in Europe?*

- *elsewhere?*

How many systems of this type have been sold in the UK (and worldwide) during the past 12 months?

Approximately how many existing database applications are there (particularly any within government?) What is the volume of text stored? How many concurrent users do the systems support?

For how long have earlier, or original, users stayed with the TIMS; or are all users (comparatively) recent?

Which are the nearest competing products available in the marketplace?

Are there any previous projects using this TIMS with which the particular vendor has been involved either inside or outside of government? Both the size and complexity of the applications are of interest.

The name and address of reference site(s) should be collected if possible. Can users be contacted, ideally in the same business area?

Does a user group exist for the product in question? Inquire:

- *whether it was formed independently of the supplier's organisation*
- *how long such a group has been in operation*
- *the number of active members*
- *the number of meetings held each year*
- *when and where meetings are held?*
- *joining/ membership fees*
- *the name, address and telephone number of the group's secretary.*

How closely does the company collaborate with any such user groups which might be established?

Product information	Sources of information other than those suggested by the product supplier can be valuable.

Chapter 10
Product credibility

Are there any independent reports and evaluations on the TIMS being considered? Can copies of any reports be made available? (If copies are not available, this may be because they contain adverse results, and a search for alternative sources may be worth while.)

User Profile

Many TIMS are intended to be accessible directly to the end-user. They do, however, normally require systems support at least during design and database creation, and in complex projects there may be long-term systems and programming involvement - typically with text acquisition, and the development of structured reports.

Who are expected to be the principal implementors of information systems and services based on the TIMS?

- *end-user staff*
- *analysts*
- *novice programmers*
- *experienced programmers*
- *others (to be specified).*

The answers to these questions may be expected to differ between traditional text and DBMS+Text products.

10.5 Documentation

Text-based information management systems require adequate documentation. Frequently products at the beginning of their life, or TIMS marketed by small organisations, appear with inadequate documentation. Others appear with large volumes of poorly structured documentation.

What information is available about the TIMS before purchase?

What documentation is available, and how well is it presented?

What manuals and other documentation are provided when the TIMS is purchased?

What other 'optional' manuals are available?

Can the documentation be copied by the user for his own use only?

What is the target audience for each manual for example management overview, system designer, application programmer, operator, etc?

Are the manuals available online?

What information is available on the technical content of the system, for example:

- *internal file formats*
- *database structure*
- *query optimisers*
- *compression and encryption methods*
- *validation mechanisms*

In the event of the supplier going out of business, what arrangements are there for access to the source code, for example is a copy of the source code lodged with an Escrow Agent?

Do existing customers use the documentation provided or is there a need to develop instructions which are specific to each installation?

10.6 Training

TIMS packages usually claim to require relatively small amounts of training, but this is not always the case. Poor quality training will predispose staff against good products and may therefore affect a project's overall success. Note that length of training required is not a sufficient guide as this will depend on the complexity of the product.

TIMS suitable for end-user development may require separate introductory courses for programmers and non-programmers.

Is training included in the purchase price of the proposed software system?

Where is training normally carried out?

Can on-site courses can be arranged?

What is the nature and amount of training normally required to operate and use the TIMS? (based on the vendor's previous experience)

What is the duration of training courses?

At which individuals is such training aimed?

Are appropriate training courses provided by the supplier?

Do any third parties offer training in the use of the TIMS?

How much computing expertise is required by attendees?

10.7 Support

Support will be required, especially when a TIMS is first introduced and before the organisation has built up its own in-house expertise. The type and level of support available will depend on the size of the supplier organisation and the number of sites they are supporting. There have been a number of instances where TIMS have enjoyed rapid market success but this has resulted in their support services being thinly stretched or staffed by poorly qualified personnel. Support quality is also likely to be dependent upon where software development is done. If all development is done overseas, then the local knowledge of the internals of the software is likely to be reduced and the time taken to fix bugs increased.

Some TIMS are purchased or marketed by UK suppliers, but not written by them. Where this is the case the level of UK support may be found wanting for newly established TIMS.

General

Where and by whom is support undertaken?

Where are the support services located?

What is the policy for supporting previous releases of the TIMS and how many versions are currently supported?

To what extent is modification by users allowed without affecting support?

How are queries and problems dealt with after installation?

For which aspects of the implementation will the supplier be responsible (for example hardware and software installation, system and data conversion, user training)?

Pre-sales

Is a demonstration available?

What are the arrangements for a trial of the TIMS?

Does the right exist to reject the product if it fails user specified acceptance tests?

Will any verbal claims and promises made by sales people be written into the standard contract?

Who will provide support/answer queries, and how accessible are they, for example by telephone, office hours only?

Installation

What maintenance and support services are available during installation of the TIMS?

Will specific personnel be allocated to this project (full time/part-time; at the beginning of, during and after implementation)?

Type and level

What maintenance and support services are available once the TIMS is operational?

How many technical support staff are supporting how many users?

How many technical support staff are available in the UK?

Does the vendor operate a 'hot-line' service for urgent user enquiries and fault reporting? If so, is the service part of a system maintenance agreement and please state:

- *the average response time*
- *the longest response time*
- *the way in which the system operates.*

How long does it take for a supplier's hot-line to answer, and how long to resolve queries?

Is there a charge for hot-line support?

Chapter 10
Product credibility

What procedures are available for reporting problems and what action and priorities are assigned to rectifying faults?

Describe the circumstances in which on-site maintenance / assistance would be given. Would such services be provided by a sales representative or by a software expert / engineer? What would be the contractual response time for a call for assistance?

Fault correction

Are details of system faults and required corrections circulated regularly to users? Is the software supplied with all corrections applied or are the corrections (fixes) supplied separately for incorporation by the user?

How are faults corrected (for example, by means of a new software issue; letter of notification; on-site assistance; or by telephone contact)?

Are new versions of the TIMS automatically sent to users?

What are the escalation procedures for fault correction? When will the Managing Director become aware of a serious fault?

10.8 Enhancements

The methods and procedures by which enhancements to software products are handled are extremely important in the context of reducing or avoiding disruption during the introduction of enhancements or improvements to the package.

What arrangements can be made for future changes which may be required by the user?

How upward compatible is the TIMS for changes to

- *the hardware?*

- *the operating system?*

Are there facilities for users to 'customise' the TIMS? If so, does this affect the supplier's willingness to warrant the compatibility of future versions?

Appraisal and Evaluation Library
Text-based Information Management Systems Volume

11 Application development

Text-based information management systems are, in themselves, valuable application development tools, and many systems have been successfully installed by end-users with only a minimum of support from computer specialist staff. Large applications, however, and those which involve the use of DBMS+Text products, often require much more formal management and may usefully apply development and productivity tools.

This chapter considers first those aspects related primarily to text-based applications; then the additional requirements of DBMS+Text products. The role of SSADM and related methodologies is considered, and finally data conversion and large volume updating

11.1 TIMS in general

There are, as yet, no generally accepted standard approaches for specification of the functional requirement of a TIMS application. Stages 1 - 3 of SSADM, namely Feasibility Study, Specification of Requirements, and Selection of Technical Options, may be used to guide these processes for TIMS. In practice a fair amount of adaptation is likely to be necessary to accommodate the indeterminate nature of many text-based information requirements. The problem is intrinsic - a text database relies to a large extent on interpretation by the user of the material, in natural language form, presented on screen, and the formal analysis often applicable to structured data is not available.

Functional design

Typical steps in the feasibility study and design stages include:

- Process and data flow diagrams for current practice;

- Projection of new processes and DFDs for known changes in requirement, and implied changes which may be deduced from analysis of the effects of TIMS use;

- Classification, description and measurement of text-based records to be placed in the database, including forming estimated of growth and update frequency;

- Identification of any of the problem aspects described in earlier chapters of this volume, and design to deal with these special effects;

- Design and rehearsal with users of the form, content and sequence of screen presentations to be used in creating, updating and searching the TIMS database; and, often

- Rapid development, testing, revision and re-trial of prototype systems or sub-systems to allow users to express their needs with some knowledge of what is realistic and practical, and to invite imaginative projection of desirable facilities possible only in an automated system.

Does the TIMS vendor provide application development aids?

Can the TIMS and the application together be made to fit in with a standard method of application development such as SSADM?

Technical options

Given a choice of technical options based on the functional requirement, and the appraisal and evaluation criteria of chapters 1 - 4 of this volume, then a number of development aids are of value in projecting disc space usage, memory requirements, response characteristics under concurrent user loads, major text acquisition timings, and communications traffic.

Does the supplier provide either technical guidelines in the documentation or computer based calculation aids for:

- *disc space usage, in the early stages, and when the database becomes mature?*

- *memory requirements based on estimated numbers of concurrent on-line users?*

- *response time projections for comparable systems?*

Chapter 11
Application development

- *resource estimation for large additions to the database, including choice of technical strategy if any?*

Case studies

Many TIMS proposals differ only in scale or detail of use from existing applications, and the use of published case studies, or of visits to established user sites may offer savings in design time, and help to provide more accurate projections of change in users' expectations.

Will the TIMS supplier provide lists of user sites where similar applications have been developed? Identify both user and technical support contacts;

Can case studies be identified in the literature using, for example, the sources identified in Annex B?

11.2 DBMS aspects

If a DBMS+Text product is being considered, then in addition to the particular text aspects of TIMS, a range of development issues concerned with the DBMS parts must be assessed. Reference should also be made to the *Appraisal & Evaluation of Database Management Systems* volume in this series, from which much of the material in this section has been adapted and summarised.

The ability of a DBMS environment to support a range of development tools (either as an integral part of the DBMS product suite, as 'add on' products, or as software from an independent software vendor) is an important aspect of evaluation. This is likely to be particularly flexible if the DBMS in question conforms to open systems standards, including the database access language SQL.

Development tools

The better DBMS development environments consist of an integrated set of tools, including a fourth generation language, a data dictionary, testing and documentation facilities. These are unlikely, at the present stage of product evolution, to extend much towards dealing with text fields and text-based retrieval.

Are any development tools provided for the text parts?

Are development tools provided for the non-text parts?

- *4GL?*

- *data dictionary?*

- *test facilities?*

- *documentation aids?*

Interactive query | The availability of interactive query facilities provided by, or compatible with, the DBMS should be investigated. Such a facility may be of use both to meet application requirements and to act as a programmers' debugging tool. Some self contained systems will have an Interactive Query Facility (IQF) as an integral part of the language. If this is the same query facility as that use for text-based searching and retrieval, then its scope will have been assessed under Chapter 2 of this volume.

Is the IQF included within the cost of the DBMS and is it an optional extra component or a separate product?

Query languages for non-DP personnel usually have an English-like syntax and in theory do not require the user to have an intimate knowledge of the database structure. Few IQFs are in practice wholly suitable for general use by non-DP personnel but 'forms' interfaces may be better, if available.

Is the IQF designed for use in a text-based retrieval context?

Is the IQF designed for use by programmers or by non-DP personnel (end users)?

What type of interface is there between the IQF and the user?

Report writer | The availability of report writing facilities should be investigated, placing particular emphasis on their adequacy for text handling. The variable length format of many text components is a particular problem in report production. Report facilities, if well designed, may significantly reduce the time taken to produce standard outputs.

Does the DBMS include a report writer facility? If so, does it deal adequately with variable length textual material in the output?

Are the sorting facilities in the report writer adequate to deal with the sequencing problems found in personal and corporate names, subject codes and extended character sets?

Is the report writer included within the cost of the DBMS, and is it an optional extra component or a separate product?

Reports can usually be specified conveniently interactively.

Are reports specified interactively or in a batch mode?

Application generators   The type, efficiency and ease of use of application development facilities, and in particular application generators (AGs), can have a significant effect on project timescales and costs. Most major database systems have some form of AG associated with them. If their usage is likely to be significant, the *Appraisal & Evaluation of Application Generators* volume in this series should be consulted.

Data dictionary   For significant system developments in the DBMS component of a dual text and structured data application, a data dictionary is highly desirable. Dictionaries which are integrated with the DBMS are more likely to be 'active' rather than 'passive' retainers of information. Most commercially significant DBMS are supported by some form of dictionary. For some systems it is an integral part or a necessary additional component.

Is the DBMS supported by a data dictionary system? Is the dictionary a prerequisite?

Does the application of the dictionary extend to the content of text fields, either as designated controlled vocabulary fields, or more generally?

How are changes propagated?

Can a data dictionary definition be 'reverse engineered' from an existing DBMS schema?

Comprehensive dictionary facilities may be expensive. For some systems, dictionaries from third party software vendors may be available.

Is the data dictionary facility included within the cost of the DBMS, is it an optional extra component or is it a separate product?

If a product from a different source from the DBMS+Text software, how does the data dictionary generate the DBMS schema?

It is desirable that the data dictionary to be used is acceptable for all system documentation. This includes documentation of conventional (non-database) files, text components of the database, and analysis documentation.

3GL development

If ancillary functions are required which are not provided by the TIMS product - stemming algorithms, access to graphics sources, etc, - the these may have to be developed in 'third generation languages' (3GL) such as COBOL, FORTRAN or C. Effective development of software of any complexity in 3GL requires tools such as test database generators and test harnesses for modules.

What specific facilities are available for application development in a 3GL environment?

End user tools

It is useful to differentiate between tools for the data processing professional and tools for the non-professional. Many relational DBMS vendors claim that their native database language is suitable for end users. In practice this is unlikely to be true; native database languages invariably require knowledge of language syntax and often require a detailed knowledge of the database structure. Better end user tools allow a menu driven form filling approach to query or report specification, and provide query views and synonyms to conceal the complexity of the database structure from the occasional user.

Chapter 11
Application development

In some TIMS products, forms or macro-based user interfaces adapted for text processing are available as an integral part of the product.

What end user tools are available?

Does the end user need to know the database structure in order to use the available tools?

11.3 Development cycle support

It is commonly recognised that the analysis, design, construction and maintenance of computer systems from an integrated set of tasks and that they should be supported by common tools; in particular, data dictionaries and more recently, analyst and programmer workbenches. In applications where DBMS+Text is proposed, integrated dictionary support is probably the most significant component, and in a Government project environment this almost certainly implies that it is desirable for the dictionary to support the Government analysis and design methodology SSADM.

Text-based information system design as a whole, however, has not proved easy to fit into SSADM or other formal methodologies, partly because the definition of user requirements proves to be volatile - that is, the user's conception of need changes rapidly and more than once as system capabilities are demonstrated. The most practical route to arrive at an early and stable requirement definition appears to be a combination of structured design of the whole, with prototyping of the main components as soon as a provisional agreement is reached on their scope.

Does the TIMS product include facilities for prototyping?

- *a micro-computer version?*
- *templates for fast database creation?*
- *facilities for logging and analysis of use of both trial and pre-production versions?*

11.4 Application documentation

TIMS products are often to some extent 'self-documenting'. This is partly in the nature of the software, but depends also on the way in which the vendor has chosen to make extra facilities available. DBMS+Text products should show in addition the standard documentation facilities of the data dictionary and any work-bench outputs.

Does the product provide documentation of database specification and construction as a by-product of installation?

11.5 Data conversion loading and migration tools

Conversion from the current system - which may be manual, and paper-based, to new systems can be a difficult business. Some database systems have emulators to allow existing applications to run in an unmodified form, accessing converted data, but this is rarely available for TIMS products. TIMS vendors may offer data conversion aids to help move data from one database environment to another.

If large volumes of text data are to be loaded, then some form of database load utility is highly desirable, although not as necessary as in a large-scale DBMS environment. Initial loading of a large database, especially one with a pointer based storage architecture, can be a very long job. Utilities may be provided which optimise this process. Such utilities provide the following types of facilities:

- Separate the parsing, reference sorting and reference list update into discrete optimised phases;

- for the DBMS part of a DBMS+Text application, build indexes only when all the base data has been stored;

- store data without resolving pointers between data elements, the pointers being resolved and stored in a later phase. Integrity checking may also be deferred until the database build is complete.

Adding large volumes of data to an existing database may be a requirement in the following circumstances:

- when databases receive periodic large increments of text records, as in, for instance, monthly

Chapter 11
Application development

archiving of transfers from office automation systems;

- during phased data take-on when initially loading a database.

Adding text and data to an existing database requires a more sophisticated approach than placing data into an empty shell.

What facilities exist to enable large volumes of data to be efficiently loaded when creating a database?

Can these facilities be used to add bulk data to an existing database?

If 'on-line' updating of text content has been specified in the requirement, is this compatible with bulk addition utilities also?

Appraisal and Evaluation Library
Text-based Information Management Systems Volume

12 Project specific requirements

Any other requirements specific to the Departmental IT Strategy and / or project, but not covered elsewhere in this volume.

Appraisal and Evaluation Library
Text-based Information Management Systems Volume

13 Costs

Cost comparison, where cost benefit analysis allows for the value of the benefits the products bring, is performed in detail for the final selection of a product from the short list of approved products. However, there is also a case for including substantial differences in costs in the higher level formulation of the short list. For this purpose (that is, initial software comparison), costing need not be done at a detailed or absolute level; approximate relative costs are sufficient.

13.1 Software

Software costs normally include a basic licence cost plus a recurrent annual maintenance charge. When prices are given it should be indicated whether these include or exclude VAT.

Is the product licensable only or can it be purchased?

How much does it cost to buy the product outright? Does this cost include a copy of the source code?

Does the product require any particular separately purchasable requisites? Or does it require extensions to operating systems or related utility software?

If image representations are involved in the application, will special purpose extension boards have to be provided for otherwise standard work-stations? Similarly, are there operating systems constraints on such work-stations when images must be displayed?

How much does it cost to rent or lease the product

- *per month?*
- *per year?*

What are the minimum and maximum rental periods? Can rentals be later offset against single purchase cost?

What are the terms for multiple copies of the product

- *on a single site?*
- *on a local area network?*
- *on multiple sites?*

Is an organisation wide licence available?

Text acquisition, vocabulary control or thesaurus software may be necessary. These may or may not be included within the standard scope and cost of the TIMS. Note also that some TIMS have many selectable (and separately purchasable) components.

Are there any other complementary software components (from any vendor source) which are required?

A reasonable level of initial installation support is useful to help gain confidence in new techniques.

What installation support is included within the purchase price? Does the price include the cost of new versions?

Is any warranty provided?

Is software support provided? If so what is the cost?

13.2 Hardware

Hardware costs associated with TIMS products to be installed on existing equipment arise mainly from the large extents of disc storage required for text and image files (Chapter 1.5). It may also be necessary to increase computer memory to allow work space for a large number of concurrent users of the text database. Communications networks should be considered also, as text-based working can result in substantial increases in traffic volumes, especially from the database node to the user.

As with software, hardware is likely to have an initial capital cost together with a recurrent maintenance cost. Costs must be considered for the system as a whole and not just the TIMS component.

What is the cost of enhancement of existing hardware (especially additional disc and / or memory) in order to support the product?

13.3 System development operation and maintenance

System associated costs vary with the type of development and tools used. TIMS themselves often rate as 4GL tools, and reduce development time and maintenance costs, but when ancillary processes such as text acquisition and report preparation are developed within the TIMS software, they may consume hardware resources during development and operation. 3GL tools may produce more efficient ancillary or special purpose efficient systems but take longer to develop and may be more expensive and difficult to maintain.

Can the product be acquired on a trial basis and if so for how long and what are the costs involved? Are these costs discounted from any subsequent purchase price?

Are 'runtime only' or 'read only' copies of the product available? If so, what is the cost? And what is excluded?

What does the maintenance contract include:

- *current version problems and fixes?*
- *minor enhancements?*
- *continuous development of the software?*

13.4 People costs

People costs are affected by factors such as the number needed, training requirements and their commercial worth. TIMS applications can incur particularly serious people costs if retrospective conversion of text and text-related material must be undertaken from printed media or microforms. Take on of new technology may require outside consultancy support which, whilst potentially cost effective, will be expensive.

Can any form of automated or semi-automated data capture (such as optical character recognition (OCR), or context sensitive terminal support) be used to limit or at least control retrospective conversion staff costs?

What is the cost of any training not provided free of charge when the product is purchased?

What is the cost of any manuals not provided free of charge when the product is purchased?

Is consultancy support available from the vendor? If so, what is the cost?

Is consultancy support available from other sources specialising in TIMS applications? If so, what is the cost?

Annex A
Criteria hierarchy

Criteria hierarchy

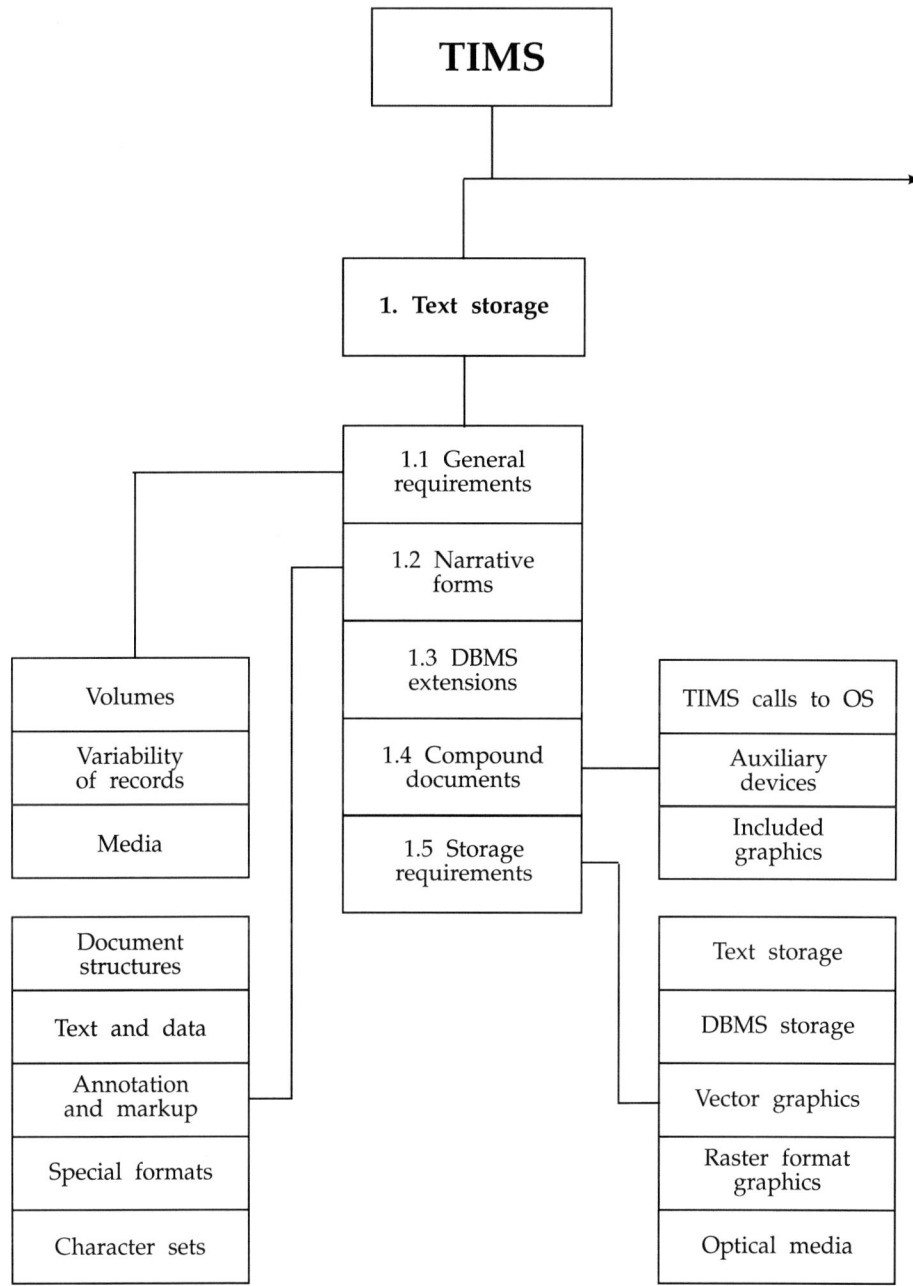

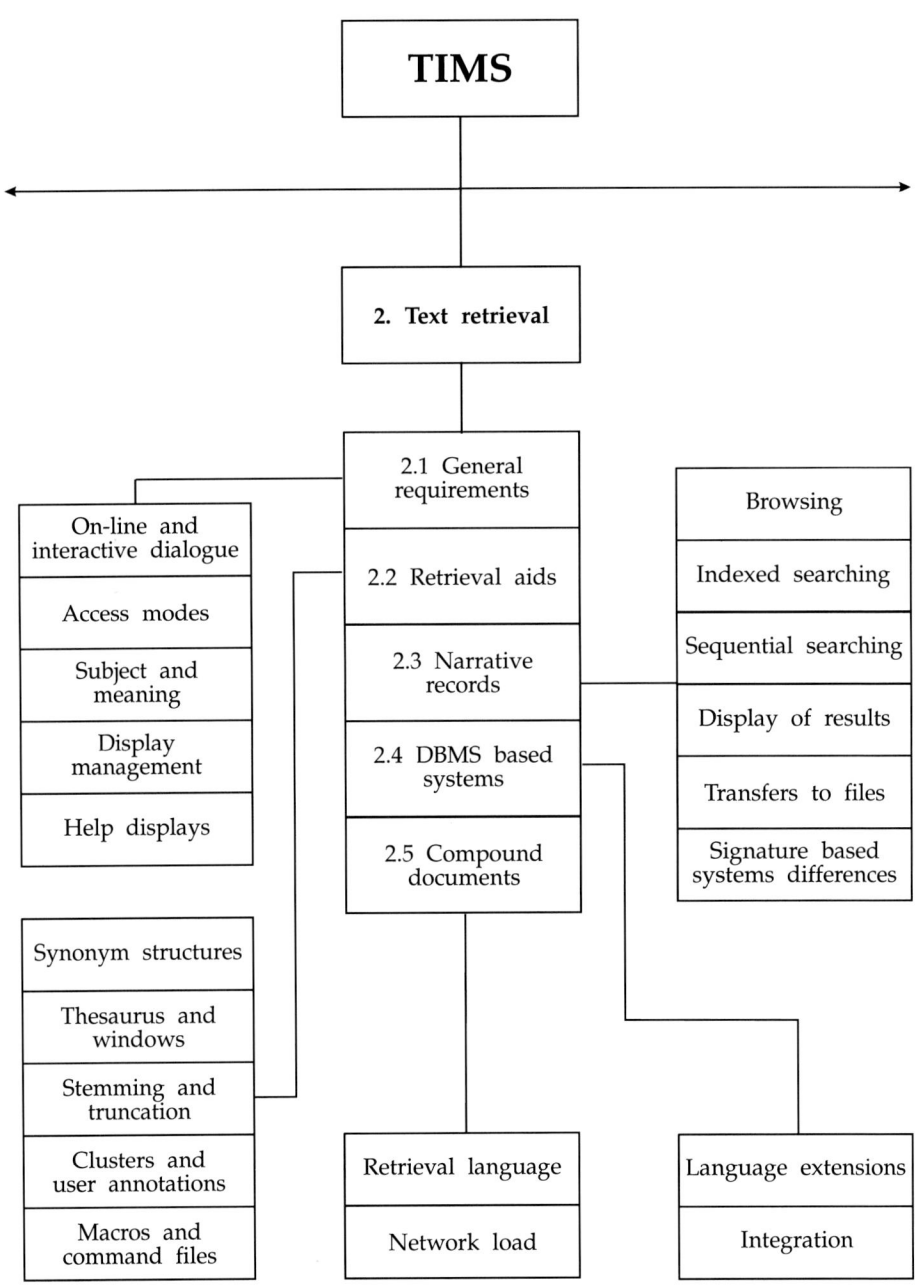

Annex A
Criteria hierarchy

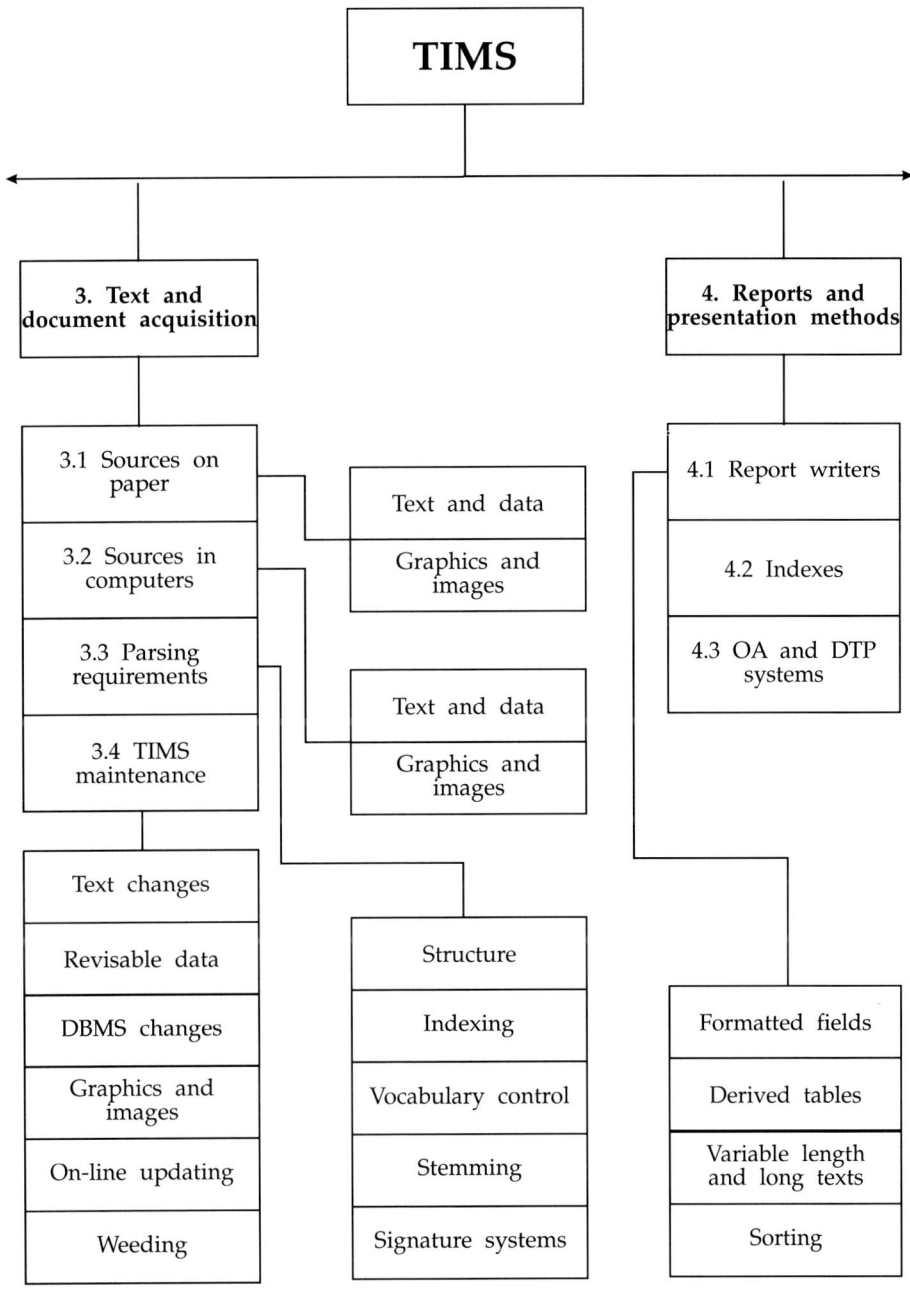

Appraisal and Evaluation Library
Text-based Information Management Systems Volume

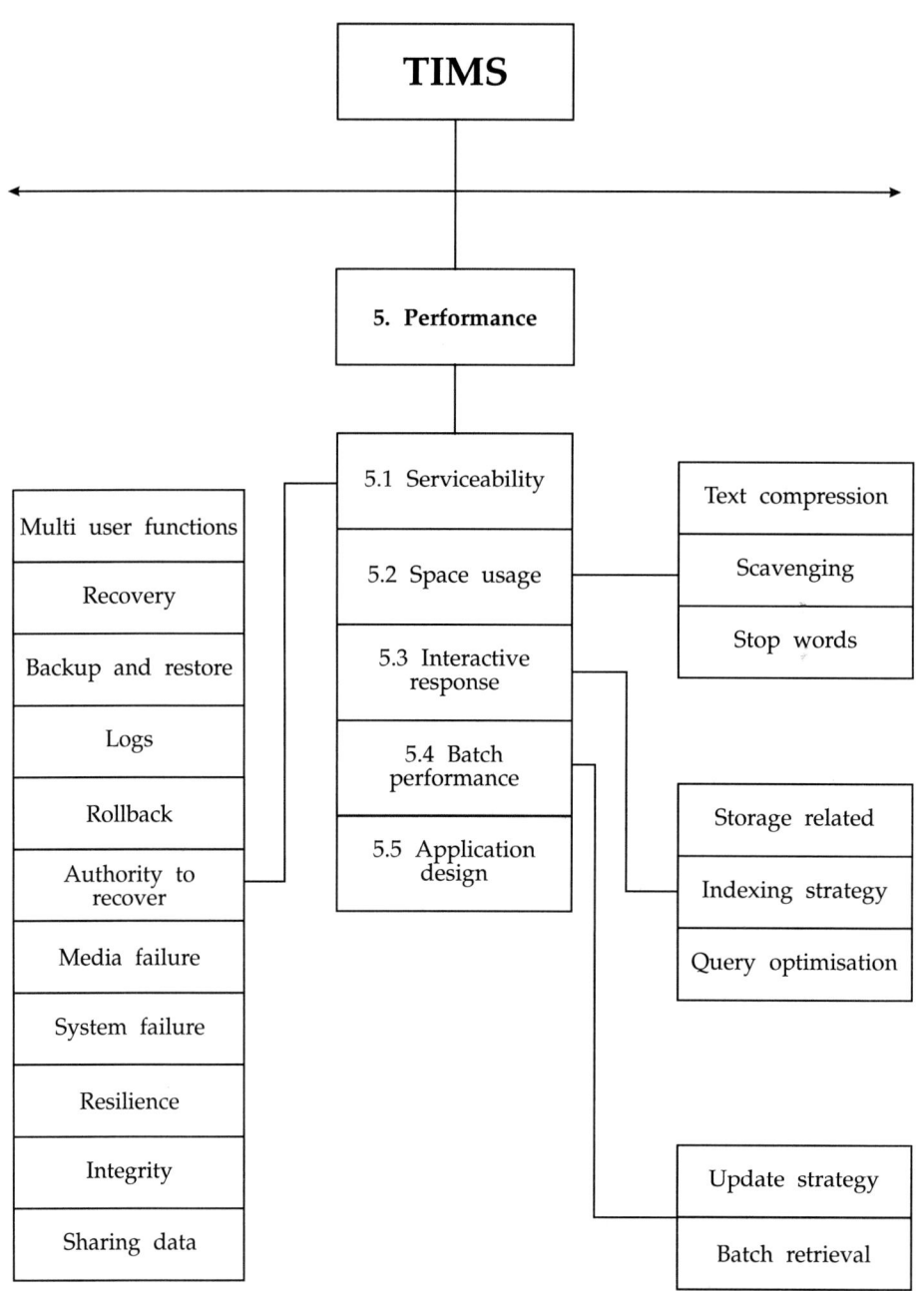

Annex A
Criteria hierarchy

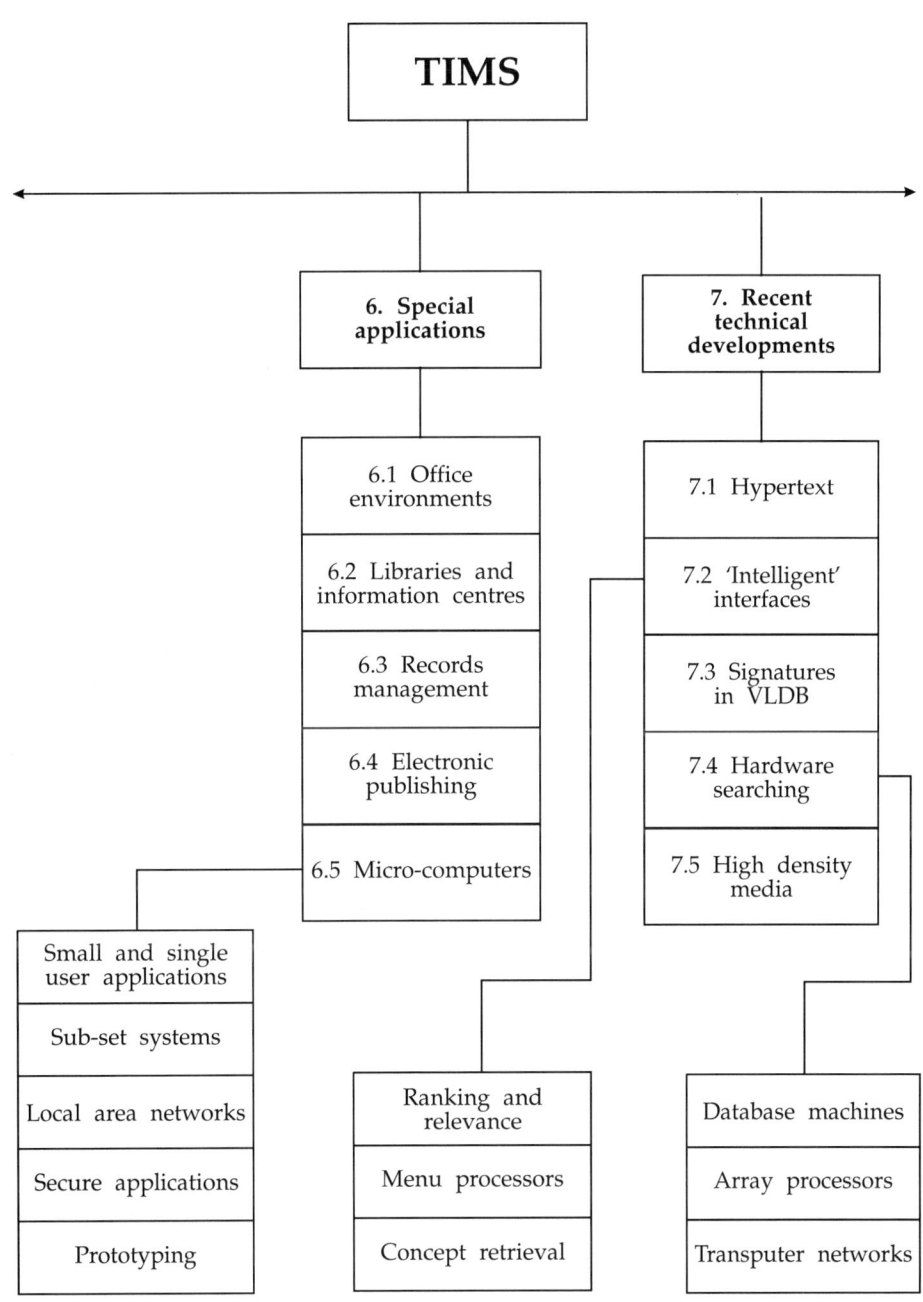

Appraisal and Evaluation Library
Text-based Information Management Systems Volume

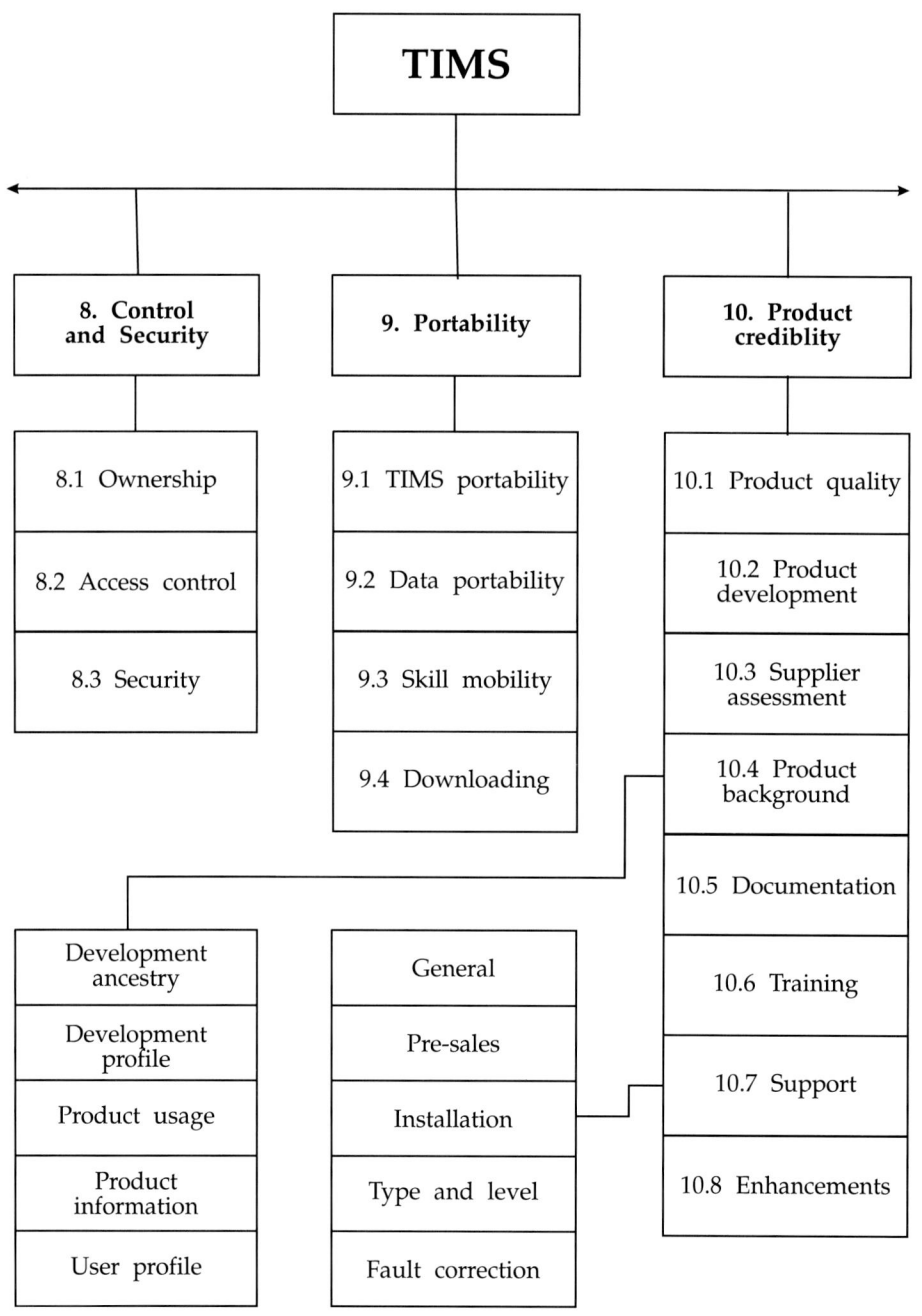

Annex A
Criteria hierarchy

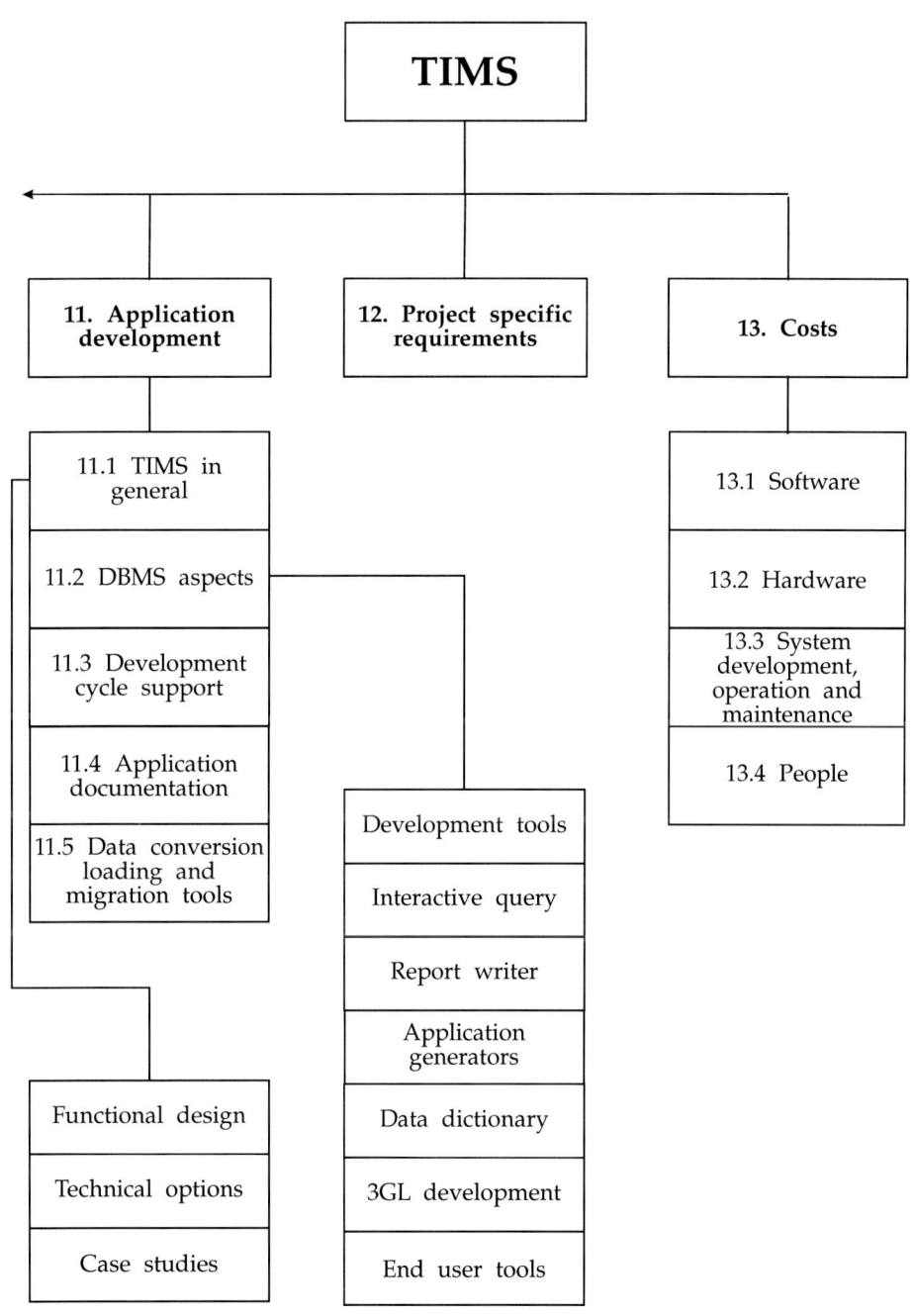

Appraisal and Evaluation Library
Text-based Information Management Systems Volume

# Sources of further information

Text-based information management systems are not generally well treated within the standard information technology literature and educational programmes, and skills and awareness in computing departments may be undeveloped. The references in this chapter are intended to provide a concise selection of key material, mostly recent, as a background to the selection and appraisal processes discussed in this volume.

They have been chosen as readily available, English language sources, with, in the case of individual papers and periodicals, a preference for European rather than North American cases where a choice has been available. The most productive on-line bibliographic sources are IFI/Plenum Information Science Abstracts, INSPEC Computer and Control Abstracts, and Library Association LISA.

B.1 Reference books and textbooks

Jean Aitchison and Alan Gilchrist, *Thesaurus construction: a practical manual*. 2nd edition. London: Aslib, 1987. (A concise and practical guide to thesaurus construction and use.)

John Ashford and Peter Willett, *Text databases and document retrieval*. Chartwell-Bratt: London, 1989 (120pp). (This is a textbook intended for students of computing and information science, for systems analysts concerned with TIMS projects, and for managers in both computer services and user departments.)

Malcolm Bain and others, *Free text retrieval systems: a review and evaluation*. London: Taylor Graham, 1989 (120pp). (This detailed account of the selection of a free text software package for the UK academic user community, by the Inter-University Software Committee, provides numerous test cases and worked examples of trial data implementations.)

C J Date, *An introduction to database systems*, Vol. 1. Fourth Edition, Reading MA: Addison-Wesley, 1986 (639pp). (Date provides a thorough and accessible account of DBMS systems in general, valuable for detailed accounts of topics such as query optimisation in relational databases. It does not deal with text-based information systems as such.)

D Alaisdair Kemp, *Computer-based knowledge retrieval.* Aslib: London, 1988 (399pp of which 48 are references). (Kemp has written a wide-ranging introduction to many aspects of information science, taking a position which assumes access to computing services as a normal resource. In the context of this TIMS volume, it is of particular value on subjects such as 'knowledge representation' and 'controlled vocabularies'.)

Robert Kimberley, ed. *Text retrieval: a directory of software.* Third edition, Aldershot: Gower, 1990 (500pp). (The third edition of this directory is the most comprehensive and thorough guide to text retrieval software currently available in the United Kingdom. It presents detailed data contributed by vendors in a standard format (but without evaluation), and summarises key features in the introductory chapters.)

Gerard Salton, *Automatic text processing: the transformation, analysis and retrieval of information by computer.* Reading, MA and Wokingham: Addison-Wesley, 1989 (530pp). (This is a textbook at senior undergraduate / post-graduate level covering the fundamentals of most aspects of text processing except computer translation of natural languages. Some sections require a basic knowledge of mathematics, but most of the material is readily accessible to readers with a computing or information science background.)

Peter Willett (ed.), *Document Retrieval Systems* - (The foundations of information science, volume 3) - London: Taylor Graham, 1988 (292pp.) (This volume has two main parts, a review of the principal research topics in its subject area during the last fifteen years; and a wide ranging set of sixteen reprints of key papers during this period.)

B.2   Conferences and journals

Three conference series have proved consistently useful in the field of text-based information systems.

Annex B
Sources of further information

At a practical and approachable level there are the annual Text Retrieval conferences in London, organised by the Institute of Information Scientists, and with proceedings published by the IIS and Taylor Graham, London.

Research work, and generally more academic applications are reported at the acm / SIGIR series of conferences on Research and Development in Information Retrieval. These are held in different European locations each year, and the proceedings are published by The Association for Computing Machinery, New York, NY.

At a less formal level, the annual meetings of the BCS/IRSG (British Computer Society / Information Retrieval Specialist Group) provide a platform for the presentation of current work, much of it by post-graduate and post-doctoral researchers concerned with the most innovative developments. This group also holds a few one day meetings each year on specific topics, sometimes jointly with other specialist groups. The annual meeting is usually in the north of England.

The literature on TIMS is very scattered, but the following journals provide a nucleus for papers covering research and applications in the United Kingdom.

Journal of Documentation, Aslib
Journal of Information Science, IIS and North Holland
Program, Aslib (library automation in particular, but note the special number on 'developments in retrieval techniques' vol. 22 no. 1, for January 1988.)

Computing science approaches are published in:

The Computer Journal, British Computer Society
Information Processing and Management, Pergamon

B.3   Selected papers

The following papers are intended to provide further reading on selected topics. So far as possible, material written in Europe, or directly applicable to a European context, has been chosen from the many papers available.

Ashford, J H, Context and application in software selection. (in) Gillman, P (ed.) *Text retrieval: the state of the art*. London: Taylor Graham, 1990. (Brief guide to software selection for various classes of application, and the consequences for support and maintenance resourcing.)

Carmichael, J W S, History of the ICL Content-Addressable Filestore (CAFS). ICL Technical Journal, vol. 4, 1985. (. . . or a number of descriptive and application papers available from all ICL offices on CAFS; ICL Defence Systems for INDEPOL.)

Doland, V M, Hypermedia as an interpretative act. Hypermedia, vol .1, no. 1, Spring 1989. (Critical review of implications for editorial responsibility in Hypertext)

Faloutsos, C, Access methods for text. ACM Computing Surveys, vol. 17, no. 1, March 1985. (Critical review of earlier research in retrieval methodology - still widely applicable.)

Pape, D L and Jones, R L, STATUS with IQ - escaping from the boolean straightjacket. Program, vol. 22, no. 1, January 1988. (Development of a document ranking extension to a widely used 'standard' TIMS product.)

Reddaway, S F and Page, R M R, High speed searching with a processor array. Microprocessing and microprogramming, vol. 24, 1988. (DAP processor applied to text retrieval)

Sacks-Davis, R and Ramamohanarao, K, A two level superimposed coding scheme for partial match retrieval. Information systems, vol. 8, no. 4, 1983. (There are several other papers by these authors on the same subject; TITAN is a derived commercial product)

Tong, R M, Appelbaum, L A, and Askman, V N, A knowledge representation for conceptual information retrieval. International Journal of Intelligent Systems, vol. 4, 1989. (Research underlying systems such as TOPIC)

Annex B
Sources of further information

Walker, S, Improving subject access painlessly: recent work on the Okapi online catalogue projects. Program, vol. 22, no. 1, January 1988 (Practical, user oriented research on interfaces to online catalogue databases, but relevant to TIMS in general.)

Printed in the United Kingdom for HMSO.
Dd. 295352, C6, 9/91, 3390/3, 5673, 162119.